The Ups and Downs of Being Round

*Nikki,
Be encouraged.
Be inspired.*

The Ups and Downs of Being Round © 2007 by Monica Jones

Author Information:

Monica Marie Jones

monicamjones@hotmail.com

http://www.myspace.com/monicamariejones

Published by:

HubBooks/Sylvia Hubbard

PO Box 27310

Detroit, MI 48227

hubbooks@yahoo.com

HubBooks.biz

313.289.8614

This is a work of fiction. Names, characters, places, and incidents either are the product of the author's imagination or are used fictitiously, and any resemblance to actual person, living or dead, business establishments, events, or locales, is entirely coincidental.

All rights reserved.

This book, or parts thereof, may not be reproduced in any form without permission.

Cover design by: Micah Funches

Book Formatting by: Sylvia Hubbard

10 Digit ISBN: 0-9774435-6-6

Author is available for speaking events and bookclub appearances. Contact monicamjones@hotmail.com for scheduling.

This book is dedicated to and made possible by the following...

The constants in my life: GOD, Mom and Jr. My nephew/God son Lil' Ron. The sisters I always wanted Monike, Renae (Sherica) and Kalita. My anchor and spiritual partner Travon. My family: Dad, Oscar, Grandma, Aunt San, Uncle Johnny, Phoenix, Aurora and Daniel. My spiritual mentors Miss Kita and Kelli. My literary mentor Sylvia Hubbard. My fitness mentor Monique Sasser. My editor Chris Campbell. My artist Micah Funches. My photographer and friend Arthur King. My surrogate dads Virgil Phillips and Marcus Webster. My professional mentor Anthony Williamson. My colleagues at the High/Scope Educational Research Foundation. My church family at Friendship Baptist Church. Decky and Close Up. Diversion Dance Troupe. People that have touched my life by giving me opportunities to minister: DeMilla, Ryan, Evangelist Cole, and Ki Ki Sheard.

All of my students over the years particularly my REACH kids and my dance students with special dedications to The Carter brothers, Tiffany, Venitta, Kaneesha, Madi, the Richards sisters and Eleza.

In loving Memory of Grandpa and Tomi Terre Hollingshed.

To those whom I did not name, write your name here_____ and know that there will be many more books where this came from.

Thank you all.

I love you.

Part One:

Childhood

"Fat Girl"

Prologue

This little piggy cried, "wee, wee, wee," all the way home

"Miss Piggy!" she yelled loud enough for all of our classmates to hear but just out of earshot of the teacher. Unable to think of a quick and clever enough comeback, I simply responded with, "shut up." Although my birth name is Madison, my own personal elementary school bully, Veronica, had dubbed me with a new title, *Miss Piggy.* The Muppets was one of my favorite shows but that didn't mean that I wanted to be one of them.

Veronica tortured me during my elementary school years. I am not sure why I was given the honor of being her daily target, but that was the case during most of my school days. It wasn't like she could kick my butt or anything; as a matter of fact, she never even tried to put her hands on me. She only beat me down with her words - which hurt more than any blow to the body ever could. Even if she did try to sock me, her fist might have gotten lost in flabby abyss. Or perhaps it would have bounced back and knocked her out. With an 140 pound frame at the age of eight, I couldn't blame her for her remark, despite the fact that she was no "skinny-mini" her darn self.

I came home in tears because of the teasing that I had endured from Veronica. Between hiccups and staggered breathing I explained the reason for my tears to my mother. "Oh sweetie, you're not fat, you're just big boned.," she said in a sorry attempt to make me feel better. I was too worked up from my crying frenzy to respond. But I thought, just how big can a bone really be? I've never seen a human skeleton in any book or on TV that had big bones, only dinosaurs.

Mom led me down the hall so that we could stand in front of the full-length mirror on the bathroom door. After placing me in front of the mirror, she stood behind me and said, "Madison, just look at those almond shaped eyes and that beautiful skin." I stared… and stared…and stared some more, yet saw nothing. As I continued my gaze, a fresh batch of tears began to gather on my bottom lids. The liquid expanded over my eyeballs blurring my vision and distorting my image in the mirror. The more I stared the more I started to look like… Miss Piggy.

Mom would always say that I was pretty. I never saw in myself what she saw in me. She wouldn't lie to me would she? She was probably just saying all of this to make me feel better or because I was her daughter. Would a mother really lie to her daughter?

Perhaps sensing my insecurities, several adults would comment on how attractive I was *going* to be when I grew up. "Your mom will have to build a fence around the house with guard dogs to keep the boys out," said Eva, my Mom's best friend who was visiting that night.

What the heck was she talking about? Was this some cruel joke that I had mysteriously become the butt of? I asked to be excused from the living room. I needed to get away from all of the compliments that Mom and Eva were showering me with. Why couldn't they just tell me the truth? If I was so wonderful, why was it that people only told me so when I was at home?

The Ups and Downs of Being Round
Monica Marie Jones

I stared in the mirror for hours trying to see the things that they saw to no avail. What I did see was a fat girl.

Daddy's Little Girl

Whenever Mom's attempts to make me feel better failed, I went to Daddy. He was in the kitchen getting dinner ready.

"Daddy, do I look like Miss Piggy?" I asked, knowing full well that he would not say yes, but in fact say something to make me feel a whole lot better than how I was feeling at present.

"I don't know who this Miss Piggy is, but unless she looks like a beautiful Belizean Jamerican princess, then no, you don't look like her." Wow, my Daddy sure had a way with words. I was feeling better already - especially after I sunk my teeth into one of the golden crisp fry cakes that he had just taken out of his big, black cast iron frying pan and placed on a piece of paper towel to drain the grease.

My daddy is from Belize, a country in Central America that borders Guatemala. If he had to check the race box on an application, society would expect him to check the Hispanic box. The truth was that his ethnicity was a beautiful mix of many rich cultures that should not be limited to a tiny box. He is a tall, thin man with beautiful skin and soft, curly tufts of jet-black hair. He is quite handsome. Mom said that back in the day all of the women wanted one of the Jenson brothers. Well she snagged one and now I was lucky enough to have Ryan Jenson as my daddy. Most nights I would fall asleep, my head snuggled between the rise and fall of his chest while we watched sitcoms like *M.A.S.H* and *Sanford and Son* on television.

The Ups and Downs of Being Round
Monica Marie Jones

After I finished the first fry cake, I quickly reached for another. The hot doughy goodness gave me a euphoric sense of comfort and peace. Dad's cooking always makes my mouth water and my stomach constantly yearn for more. Every night he prepares an assortment of Central American cuisine - foods such as fry cake, tortilla, pasta, served with an ever-present heaping pot of white rice. Many of the things that he cooked were fried with shortening. Shortening, like lard, was a big vat of a white thick and creamy substance that later in life I learned was nothing more than animal fat. I didn't even know that lighter alternatives such as canola or olive oil existed until I was well into adulthood.

I sat there in the kitchen with dad and munched on fry cakes until dinner was ready. When I fixed my plate I piled it high with food and topped it with two more fry cakes. When I finished that plate, I got seconds without another thought about it. Halfway through my second plate I realized that I was getting full so I pushed my plate a way to take a breath. Just as I was about to get up, Mom stopped me by saying, "I know you are not about to waste all of that food. There are kids in other countries that are starving. We can't afford to be wasting food like that. You'd better clean your plate young lady." Even though I felt as if I was about to explode, I did as I was told. As soon as I was done I waddled to my bedroom, plopped on to my bed and went straight to sleep.

My first love: Food

I was awakened from sweet slumber by the squeaks and creaks that Mom's approaching footsteps made as she walked across my wooden bedroom floor. When I opened my eyes she greeted me with two thick slices of Jamaican hard dough bread slathered with butter and jelly. I quickly gobbled them down without any remorse as the crumbs and globs of jelly that adorned my pajamas and bed sheets.

"Are you feeling any better this morning sweetheart?" she asked sincerely.

"Yeah." I lied. The food had given me temporary satisfaction, but I was dreading going to school to face another day.

Mom is from Jamaica but she doesn't cook much. Where she lacked in the culinary department, Grandma and Auntie Lela would make up for it. They were always preparing a West Indian feast of curry goat, fried plantain, calaloo (spinach), rice and peas, ackee with salt fish, and the list goes on and on. Food was my first love. I ate when I was sad. I ate when I was happy. I ate when I was bored. My favorite time to eat was just after Mom came home from grocery shopping. Whether I was hungry or not I wanted to taste each and every new food that she brought into the house.

There was always an abundance of food and a whole lot of cooking going on. You would think that with this type of lifestyle everyone in the family would be plump, but this was not so. I was the only one. Mom still had some of her pregnancy weight after giving birth to my little brother, Ryan Jr, but at least she had an excuse. What was mine?

Mom looked good despite her pregnancy weight, but continued to constantly diet. She had a small frame and a nice figure so her constant dieting made me feel like I really needed to lose weight. Even though I was a child, I was bigger than she was. Seeing her diet all the

The Ups and Downs of Being Round
Monica Marie Jones

time while I was growing up taught me that you have to be skinny to be pretty and feel good about yourself.

That day when Mom got home from work she asked me the usual questions about my day as I helped her clean the house.

"How was school today Maddy?" she would ask.

"It was okay." I lied. "We talked about careers because we are having career day next month."

"Oh, that's nice. What do you want to be when you grow up?"

Without much thought or hesitation I answered, "skinny." She laughed nervously. It looked like she was not sure whether to laugh or cry. I didn't understand her confusion though because I was dead serious about my answer. After that we continued to clean the house in silence.

I wanted to be skinny when I reached adulthood. I longed to be skinny with really straight hair just like the women on TV. I wanted to be able to wear a bikini and swing my hair from side to side as I ran down the beach barefoot. Sometimes when no one was watching, I would put on my Wonder Woman underwear set, which was my bikini. Then I would drape a towel over my head, which represented my long straight hair. The shaggy carpet in the house would be the hot sand squishing between my toes as I ran on the imaginary beach.

After helping to clean house, I would play imaginary beach games with myself to get rid of boredom. I would run from my imaginary man that was chasing me along my make believe beach. I would look back to catch a glimpse of him. But when I would turn around my fantasy would come to a screeching halt as my face met abruptly with the wall. My front tooth was instantly knocked out upon impact. So as if being fat wasn't hard enough, I was toothless to boot.

You're a BIG girl now

Dad couldn't swing me around anymore like he used to when I was little and Mom couldn't pick me up anymore. I yearned for these simple pleasures because I was still at an age when this was the way that parents played with their children. That weekend my friend Sharla came over to spend the night and dad swung her around and around, then it was my little brother Ryan's turn to experience the joy. All I could do was look on in awe.

Since I didn't have the comfort of my parents being able to pick me up and hold me when I needed solace, I sucked on my pacifier until well after my sixth birthday. A week later I lost it while I was playing with Ryan in the attic. With my pacifier gone, I was left with a massive overbite and all the more reason to pacify myself with food. I always had the urge to suck or chew on something. This made me pick up a few other bad habits. I started sucking my thumb. When I got scolded for that, I would bite and chew on my nails until they bled.

Overload

Our house in Detroit was within walking distance of the Michigan State Fair. Every summer the family would walk there to enjoy a day of shows, rides and elephant ears. This particular summer was no different. I had run myself ragged because I was so excited. The colors, sights, and sounds had sent me into sensory overload. When it was time to go home, I was too tired to walk. I knew that there was no way Dad could carry me so I asked Mom if I could sit in the stroller for a while to rest my tired legs. These were the days when

The Ups and Downs of Being Round
Monica Marie Jones

strollers were a thin sheath of fabric on four small wheels and handles that looked like candy canes without the stripes. They could also fold like an umbrella for easy carrying. With a reluctance that I didn't understand at the time, she allowed me to sit in the stroller until I would have to trade with Ryan Jr.

The relaxed situation lulled me into a drowsy state, until I was suddenly awakened by a loud CRACK. I found myself on the cement amongst the broken glass and cigarette butts - the stroller wheel had given under my weight and was sitting on a gangster lean in three-wheel motion. It wasn't because I was too old to be in a stroller. It was because I was too heavy. To make me feel better, my mother quickly helped me up and brushed me off. Then she scolded the stroller, "this cheap piece of crap!"

We all walked home on sore feet in silence.

CHAPTER ONE

Back to the Beginning: The first day of school

Before I began going to school, I was a fairly happy child. But that all changed shortly after my first day of school. The bothersome days of being bashed for my bulges began way before my personal bully Veronica had come into the picture.

In the fall it was time for me to start kindergarten. I was so excited because I already knew how to read and was ready and eager to learn more. I was also looking forward to the new friends and playmates that Mom told me I would meet at my new school. I had gotten so much love and praise at home that I thought I was a wonderfully normal child. I expected the same acceptance and approval from my soon to be classmates.

The night before the first day of school I could barely sleep because I was so anxious. I sharpened my brand new set of Smurfs pencils and laid them in my Rainbow Bright pencil box next to my big blue eraser and an eight pack of crayons. I placed my pencil box and my new metal Strawberry Shortcake lunch box into my pink and purple backpack. I laid out my tan corduroy skirt with cream-colored knit tights, my new monogrammed sweater vest, a cream mock turtleneck with Buster Brown penny loafers. I made sure that there was a shiny new penny in each of them. Mom had done my hair in fresh cornrows with an array of colorful beads on the ends. I convinced her to let me borrow her silk hair bonnet so that every strand of hair stayed in place, while I slept. Once I checked and

The Ups and Downs of Being Round
Monica Marie Jones

double-checked that everything was in place I got under the covers of my pink canopy bed and tried to imagine the different happy encounters that I would have at my first day of school.

The reception that I did get was far from what I had expected. As far as I knew, based on my family's perception, I was pretty, smart, and had a vibrant personality. I didn't know that I was portly until I actually started school. The other kids were eager to inform me of that.

My next-door neighbor is the same age as me. Her name is Jaynelle. Our parents arranged for us to walk to school together since it was only at the end of the block. She was very nice. I could tell instantly that we would hit it off as great friends. She had forty pigtails in her hair with variously colored "I Love Jesus" barrettes attached to each end. She had on a khaki colored jumper with knit tights just like mine. But it would have taken three of her legs to make one of mine because she was skinny.

Jaynelle and I were both extremely nervous, so stayed together, being glued to the hip like Siamese twins all day. Everything went well until we stumbled into the path of the class jokester. He was even thoughtful enough to go as far as to serenade us with our own personal theme song, with lyrics made especially for us:

Fatty and skinny went to bed,
Fatty rolled over and skinny was dead.

I guess I was fatty. Granted, the song was directed to the both of us as a package deal, but I took it far more personally. I was tired of being fatty. I wanted to be skinny. Being fatty wasn't fun. I was an outgoing child before I started school, but once the other children

The Ups and Downs of Being Round
Monica Marie Jones

made fun of my weight, I became shy so as not to bring too much attention to myself.

I reasoned that if they didn't notice me, they couldn't tease me. I would keep my mouth shut all day at school. I was so quiet that by the time I opened my mouth, my breath would pour out like hot lava and smell horribly from keeping my breakfast and lunch trapped in the back of my mouth all day. If being overweight and toothless didn't cause enough persecution, I had a mean case of halitosis as well. To cope, I kept my head buried in books. I figured since I couldn't impress people with my appearance, I would try to gain their praises with good grades. That night and every night thereafter, I got down on my knees and prayed.

Dear God,

I pray for all of my friends and family. I thank you for them and pray that you watch over them. I ask that you forgive me for my sins. Thank you for today, but I pray that tomorrow will be a better day. I pray that no one will talk or pick on me. Thank you for giving me Jaynelle as a friend because if I didn't have her I would not have any friends at school. You are a miracle worker. I love you.

Amen.

I learned a lot of things in church including how to pray. That helped me to deal with the torment that I faced at school. At Sunday school we learned about the Trinity. The Trinity was the Father, the Son, and the Holy Spirit. I was intrigued by that lesson, so as a result I created three imaginary friends in my mind that I could talk to every night. The picture of the father and the son in my head were an older and younger version of the pictures of Jesus that I had seen at church.

The Ups and Downs of Being Round
Monica Marie Jones

The Holy Ghost was a lady. Every night before I went to bed I would talk to them about my problems before I prayed. It gave me comfort to know that someone was listening. The support of Jaynelle and my three imaginary friends helped me to make it through that first year of school.

CHAPTER TWO

My first diet

That next year when I went to my pediatrician for a check up, my doctor told Mom that I weighed too much for my age. She suggested that I be put on a diet. When we got home that afternoon Mom decided to hide all of the treats that she usually let me eat. It didn't bother me at first because we had just had lunch at McDonalds. The reality hit me when she didn't let me get seconds at dinnertime or dessert that night. I was so mad so I went to my room and read until I knew she was asleep. I made my first move on "mission munchies," once I was sure everyone in the house was sleep.

I scoured the house for snacks, looking in all of the closets, the basement, the pantry, and in the highest cabinets, but to no avail. I checked the bathroom, in one last ditch effort, but found nothing until I got to the medicine cabinet. I came across a blue box and looked inside. Jackpot! The box contained squares of chocolate that looked like a Hershey bar. She thought she was slick by hiding it in the medicine cabinet.

She always told us never to take any medicine unless she gave it to us. I had already been scolded severely once before for taking medicine without her permission.

She would always give us chewable Flintstone's vitamins and explain that they were important to make us stay healthy. I loved the

The Ups and Downs of Being Round
Monica Marie Jones

tasty and colorful assortment of pills that were shaped like the different characters on the cartoon.

I wanted my Mom to be just as healthy as us so I asked her why she didn't take the Flintstone's vitamins. She explained that those vitamins were for kids and that she took grown up vitamins. A few weeks later I saw her taking some pills. They were in a clear plastic capsule with colorful tiny dots inside that looked like miniature versions of the candy sprinkles that she put on top of our ice cream. I asked her what they were and she said that they were vitamins.

She always treated me like I was an adult, so I made the adult decision that it was due time for me to switch over to grown up vitamins. One day before she got home from work, I climbed onto the sink and got her vitamins out of the medicine cabinet. I opened the plastic capsule and emptied the colorful dots into my hand. I poured them into my mouth. I was disappointed that they did not taste sweet like the Flintstone's vitamins or like candy sprinkles. I quickly washed them down with some water to get the horrible taste out of my mouth.

When mom came home from work, I raced to meet her at the door. I assured her that I was officially a big girl now because I had taken grown up vitamins all on my own. The proud and approving look that I expected from her instead was a scowl mixed with anger and concern. "Maddy, what are you talking about? What grown up vitamins did you take?" I ran to the bathroom and grabbed the box that contained the vitamins to show her. She snatched the box from me and whooped my butt. Every whack on my bottom coincided with a word that explained why taking those vitamins were wrong.

The Ups and Downs of Being Round
Monica Marie Jones

I came to find out that those pills were not vitamins at all. I had taken a popular diet pill called Dexatrim. It was not safe for kids to take them. After that butt whooping, she thought that the medicine cabinet would be the last place that I would ever want to look. Clever, but she thought wrong. I quickly devoured the whole box of chocolates. I closed the box and placed it back in the cabinet exactly where I found it in an attempt to cover my tracks. I quietly tiptoed back to my room. Before I entered the room I stopped, looked right and left. I wanted to make sure the coast was clear before I entered my room and went to sleep.

Brrrrplgurrglplip! A little over an hour had passed when a massive rumbling in my belly woke me up. I then felt a tidal wave of pressure crash against my bowels. I clenched my booty tight, putting my hand there for extra support. I carefully walked to the bathroom so as not to cause the volcano in my behind to erupt before I got to the toilet. As soon as my butt cheeks hit the toilet everything I ate over the last week as well as all of the fluids in my body rushed forth from my bunghole with the pressure of a fireman's hose. I was sweating, sore, dehydrated and I feeling empty.

This was one time I was happy to have some weight on me because if I were skinny, my belly button would have been touching my back. With what little strength I had left I cried, "Mooommmmyyyyyy!" She rushed from her bedroom into the bathroom. "What's wrong baby?" she asked with a groggy yet sincere look of concern on her face. In my most dramatic whiny baby voice I answered, "I've got the runs Mommy."

"What did you eat?"

The Ups and Downs of Being Round
Monica Marie Jones

"I don't know."

"Well let me get you something to make you feel better"

She went into the medicine cabinet in search of the Pepto-Bismol. As she was searching through the contents of the cabinet she picked up the blue box to move it out of the way and noticed that it was unusually light. Although my head was down, I sensed her hesitancy and cringed at the thought of being found out. She opened the box and found that it wasn't just light, it was empty. As she closed the box she noticed a small brown finger print on the outside of it.

"Maddy, I know you didn't eat all of these laxatives." She said sternly.

"What?" I asked weakly.

"You heard me. Did you eat these laxatives?" She said raising her voice.

"What are laxatives?" I asked innocently.

"Did you eat the chocolates in this box?"

I was quiet

"Oh, so now you don't know how to talk?"

Again, silence.

"Well if you did eat these chocolates, that explains why you've got the runs. Maddy these are laxatives, not candy. They make you go to the bathroom when you are constipated."

"What is con-sti-pa-ted?" I said barely able to pronounce the word.

"When you are constipated, you can't go to the bathroom."

Using the little fluid that I had left in my body I began to cry. I guess that's what I get for being so greedy. When I couldn't use the bathroom anymore, mom gave me crackers, a large glass of water, and some Vaseline to slather on my sore booty hole before she sent me to my room.

"I guess I don't need to bother punishing you for this since you have clearly punished yourself enough. Now, I bet you won't go snooping for snacks in the middle of the night anymore, will you?" she said desperately trying to mask her sly grin, which tumbled over into a quiet giggle. After I finished my crackers and water, I went to sleep on my stomach that night.

Food fiend

Unfortunately I didn't learn my lesson from that "butt" shattering experience. It was painful, but it was not enough to make me stop wanting food. If anything it made me want food more just because I couldn't have it. I had always been stubborn that way. I got in the habit of stopping at Ted's Penny Candy Store every day after school. I would spend all of my allowance on candy, chips, and pop. I would eat all that I could on the way home to get rid of the evidence. When I couldn't eat it all, which was rare, I would take it home and hide it in a shoebox under my bed. Mom just couldn't understand why I was not losing any weight. It baffled her that I was gaining more.

After a year had passed, my mom realized that her efforts at reducing my food intake were not successful. She felt that it was time to try a different route. In a second attempt to help me shed the excess baggage, mom did research on extra curricular physical activities that I could do to get more exercise. She ended up signing me up for dance lessons at the local dance studio, Feet in Motion. I was in a beginner class that taught ballet, tap, jazz, modern dance, and gymnastics. We

The Ups and Downs of Being Round
Monica Marie Jones

had to wear a leotard and tights to class. This meant I had to actually appear in public looking like a Honey Baked Ham in an outfit that looked to me like nothing more than cheap pantyhose and a bad swimsuit. To make matters worse we had to choose between white and ballet pink, colors that had no slimming effect whatsoever.

On the first day of dance class I walked into the small studio with shiny wooden floors. I sucked in my stomach as I entered the studio as if it would actually make me look smaller. There were two girls there when I arrived. I sat alone in a corner and watched as each new girl entered waiting to see if by chance there might be another girl my size or bigger. There was none. The teacher had us spread out on the floor and began teaching us the five foot positions of ballet. A few more latecomers trickled in but by the time we got to third position all of the students had arrived. It was no surprise to me that I was the largest girl in the class.

I found ballet and modern dance to be pretty boring but enjoyed the faster pace and more stylish movements of tap and jazz dance. Aside from being nearly twice the size of my classmates, I blended into the background very well until it was time for gymnastics. A thin, yet strong and muscular male teacher with tight spandex pants and a cut off t-shirt entered the room. I grossed out by the fact that I could see the bulge in his crotch. He told us to call him Johnny. This was the first time I didn't have to address a teacher by Mr. or Miss. He explained that we would learn a whole lot today. He wanted to see what everyone's ability was and he wanted us to get right to learning most of the stunts so that we could practice them each week to get better at performing them.

The Ups and Downs of Being Round
Monica Marie Jones

We learned how to do back bends, splits, cartwheels, round-offs, front and backhand springs. Johnny demonstrated each flip then told us to give it a try. He told us not to worry about falling or hurting ourselves because he would spot us. I doubted that he could spot me, but since he was the teacher and he had pretty big muscles I decided to let my guard down and trust him. I was fairly decent at all of the basic moves. I just had trouble with the front and backhand spring. When it was my turn to try the back handspring I wasn't afraid. I saw Johnny basically flipping kids without them having to put forth any effort. It looked so fun! Everyone was giggling hysterically and bouncing all around the room while they waited for their turn. I was having such a great time that I forgot for an instant that I was overweight.

Johnny seemed so strong that I just let myself go in his arms as if I was dong the dead man's float in a swimming pool. I always felt weightless, light, and free when I was immersed in water. Suddenly my imaginary swimming pool was drained of its water in four seconds flat when I felt myself hitting the mat with a thud. Johnny quickly helped me up and apologized. I was ready to go at this point but he insisted that *I* try again. Like *I* was the one that dropped *me*. He called his assistant in to stand on the other side to help him spot me. They really did not need to make all of this fuss over me. Besides, no one else needed two people to spot them.

Johnny told me to jump and reach for the sky on the count of three. One. Two. Three. I closed my eyes and jumped. I felt some airtime then felt my feet hit the ground safely. I was just about to take a deep sigh of relief when I remembered that half way through my hang time I felt my knee hit something. When I opened my eyes and

The Ups and Downs of Being Round
Monica Marie Jones

looked to the left I saw that Johnny was fine. When I looked to my right I was shocked to see Johnny's teenaged assistant on the ground. I gathered from the chatter of two girls close to me that my knee had hit him in the head halfway through my backhand spring. Hearing all of the commotion, the director came in and helped the poor teen out of the room to get an ice pack. I used the upheaval to my advantage by slowly tip toeing into the background. When I was sure no one was looking, I slid through the door and escaped into the dressing room. I hid behind one of the curtains until my mother and the director found me there crying well after everyone else had gone home.

The next day at school the assignment in gym class was to run a mile around the playground. "Oh great," I thought. As if the disastrous drama of last night wasn't enough, now I had to try to run a mile. I had never attempted to run a few feet and now I was expected to run a mile. I hoped that the friction that was about to occur between my thighs wouldn't start a fire.

Ten times around the playground was a mile and it was timed. The expected timeframe to complete the mile for a healthy child was around 12 minutes. When Mr. Donovan blew the whistle to begin, I took off with all of my might. I had never run a mile before, but I figured it was worth a try. About 45 seconds after my start, I began sweating profusely and gasping for air, yet kept going. I walked, jogged, ran, trotted, skipped, and galloped. I tried any movement that my body could muster to keep pushing forward. I watched my classmates pass me by one by one. As students began to finish, I was only on the fifth lap, which meant I was only halfway done. Eventually, everyone finished except for me, and I still had two laps to

The Ups and Downs of Being Round
Monica Marie Jones

go. I was determined not to stop, as long as I still had an erg of energy left in my body.

The class stood by and watched with mixed emotions scattered across their faces as I completed my mile - alone. Some people had a hopeful look in their eyes as if they were trying to will me along, but most looked on with impatience and disgust. I continued to push on, though I only had enough energy left to produce a staggered walk. Drenched with perspiration I approached the finish line, elated that I had completed the mile, yet feeling defeated at the same time. I felt that I had jeopardized my grade, held the class up, and upset Mr. Donovan. I braced myself for the insults that were sure to follow.

Mr. Donovan looked at me sternly and said, "Class, Madison is an excellent example of what it means to try your best and never give up." Had I heard him correctly? Was I actually being praised for my horrible performance at the mile run? I was speechless. I searched my mind for the right words as Mr. Donovan reached into his pocket and pulled out a pack of Strawberry Now and Laters candy. He handed them to me as a reward for my perseverance. Just as I began to feel excitement over my accomplishment, I overheard one of my classmates whisper to another, "Her fat butt know she don't need no Now and Laters." Of course Mr. Donovan didn't hear it. None of my teachers ever seemed to hear the cruel things that my classmates would say to me.

I was happy for the reward, but I felt like a loser. I hadn't given up, but I finished last, using all of the power that I could gather. During childhood, when I should have been the most active, it took me twenty-five minutes to complete a mile. Ironically, my reward would

The Ups and Downs of Being Round
Monica Marie Jones

be the one thing that had led me to my downfall - food. Rewards for perseverance were good, but the truth was that I was overweight, out of shape at only eight years old. When Mr. Donovan wasn't looking, I gave my Now and Laters to the nearest person who hadn't teased me that day.

Everyday after school, instead of playing outside with the other children, I opted to stay and immerse myself in the fantasy world of adult novels. Today was no different. I was especially fond of the freaky ones. Eating and reading voraciously were the highlights of my day. This was my daily routine. I loved going through mom's books and novels. I would pick out the ones with the most interesting pictures on the cover. *Elvis and Me*, and *I Tina* were among my favorite adult novels. When I felt like being a kid again I read *Sweet Valley Twins*.

Reading helped me to escape from the torment of my real life. For the hours that I had become engulfed in my reading, I was able to leave this cruel world and become part of another. Or I could find comfort in reading about someone who had it worse off than I did. It was my choice whether I wanted to be one of the characters or just an outsider looking in. I would read myself to sleep then awaken to the harsh world – which was my realty.

I found myself constantly making plans to make the day to day teasing that I suffered more bearable. I quickly found that using humor would disguise my feelings of unhappiness. I could laugh with them, or even play defense by cracking a joke about myself before they got a chance to. There's no harder thing to do than to laugh when

The Ups and Downs of Being Round
Monica Marie Jones

you really feel like crying, or trying to beat others to the punch of making a fool of yourself.

Either way it lessened the pain of the constant teasing. So in a strange masochistic sort of way, it worked for me.

When my classmate Carla asked me to join her on the see saw at recess I knew that her small frame was not enough to hoist my large body off of the ground. If I was fonder of Carla, I might have given her the joy of using my weight to hoist her up and down while I barely left the ground. Every now and then I would do that for Sharla or Jaynelle but Carla was no one special. In fact, I recall a time where someone cracked a joke about my weight and she laughed.

"Girl, unless you want to learn how to fly, I don't think that it would be a good idea for you to get on the see saw with me." Although I ached to feel the elation of my body flying weightlessly into the air as my end went up, I knew that it was an unrealistic goal to aspire to. The only way that it was possible would be if I got on there with an adult who weighed more than me, which at this point was becoming hard to find. So I cracked joke after joke about what a mistake it would be for me to get on the teeter-totter. Carla looked at me hesitantly not knowing whether to laugh, so I burst out in a fake guffaw to let her know that it was okay to join in laughing at me. My newfound sense of humor was a slight buffer, but did nothing to make my anguish relent.

CHAPTER THREE

My first crush

The teasing and jokes continued well into the summer after fourth grade. That summer Ryan Jr and I went to day camp. While at camp I took a liking to the most popular boy there, Tre. Tre was my first crush. He was older, but that didn't stop the intense feelings that I had for him. He was all that I would talk about when we got home at night. One night mom, Ryan Jr. and I were lying in her king sized bed, listening to my incessant musings about Tre.

Finally Ryan Jr interrupted my senseless banter to say, "he asked about you."

My jaw dropped in astonishment. When I was able to talk again, I begged and pleaded for Ryan Jr to tell me what he said. After some thought, Ryan Jr. said, "He asked me who you were, and I said that you were my sister." That was not good enough for me; I poked and prodded to get more information out of him and when he didn't offer any, I made up my own fanciful scenarios about why he may have wanted to know who I was.

Once I was done with my whimsical chatter, I asked Ryan Jr. to replay the entire situation step-by-step with more detail. I needed specifics so that I could replay the fantasy over and over in my head before I went to sleep that night. By doing that I felt could will the situation into my dreams.

That's when Ryan Jr, the 5 year old innocent spitting image of my father, dropped the bomb on me. He cut me short saying, "okay,

The Ups and Downs of Being Round
Monica Marie Jones

okay, he never asked me about you, I just told you that because I know that you really like him and I thought that it would make you happy." I felt my heart drop into the pit of my stomach and curdle in its acid. My sweet, blameless little brother felt that he had to lie to me to make me feel happy. I was hopeless. The truth was that Tre had no idea that a little porker like me existed. Why would he want to be with the plump girl that everyone teased? I had had about all that I could stand.

That night instead of fantasizing about Tre, I fantasized about a smaller version of myself. I pictured what life would be like if I was thin. How would people treat me? What would I wear? Would boys like me? I had always been a creative and imaginative child but all that I could see that night was what I saw in the mirror everyday. That night, I dreamt that I was in front of a huge mirror wearing all black. My body kept expanding until my image was too large to be reflected in the mirror. Before long I was only seeing all black. I was too big to fit inside of my subconscious. I tried my best to scream but nothing would come out. Finally I woke up in tears and a cold sweat when I realized at that moment I had to make a change in my life. A few things happened all on their own the year that I turned ten that did indeed change my life…

The Transformation

I loved my father. In my eyes he could do no wrong, but mom's eyes saw a different man. Mom saw an alcoholic. Smirnoff Vodka was his best friend, straight no chaser. Mohawk Vodka was his pal when he was low on cash. If he had only had a forty-ounce or two of Colt 45 he was not drunk, just tipsy. We could always tell if he had a drink when he had that look in his eye - a cock eyed look where one

The Ups and Downs of Being Round
Monica Marie Jones

iris would be higher than the other making it appear as though he had a slight case of "lazy eye." He was not a raging, loud, rambunctious alcoholic who beat his wife and kids. Rather he was more of a silent alcoholic, too drunk to get up, go to work, and provide for his family. Mom got tired of lying to his bosses and feeling like she was raising three children when she had only given birth to two.

When mom and dad's divorce was final, he moved to Miami with his brother. The divorce wasn't hard or messy - no one put up a fight. Ryan Jr. and I were welcomed and encouraged to visit him anytime we wanted to. The act of divorce in itself was not traumatizing, it was having to watch *M.A.S.H* and *Sanford and Son* alone that hit me the hardest. I no longer found humor watching those shows in lonely solitude. After that night, I never watched either show again. I missed my father dearly. He called me his number #1 daughter, and although I was his only daughter, the title made me feel special. He was the only man in my life that loved me just as I was no matter what, and now he was gone. The only good that came of the situation was that there were no longer any more home cooked meals full of flour and fat. The food was delicious and I missed the rich taste of it, but its content was taking its toll on our bodies, mine in particular.

That same year, Oprah Winfrey lost 60 pounds. Mom and I lay on the bed that day and watched Oprah lug 60 pounds of animal fat out in a little red wagon to show the equivalent of the weight that she had lost. It didn't matter how or why she did it, but it was enough to inspire us.

The Ups and Downs of Being Round
Monica Marie Jones

Most other girls my age wanted to be like Janet Jackson or Whitney Houston, I however wanted to be like Oprah Winfrey. She was my hero - smart, articulate, beautiful, and confident. Everyone loved her, no matter what color her skin was, or what size her body was. Even though she was just a talk show host, she really helped people. That's how I wanted to be when I grew up. Thanks to her inspiration, Mom and I began our diet. We stopped eating junk food and started exercising. I started working harder in dance class, taking the lessons seriously. We replaced kool-aid with water. Dad's rich cooking was replaced with small-portioned TV dinners and microwave burritos. Mom started exercising in the house and her drive and persistence motivated me to follow her lead. Each day I played outside with my friends until the streetlights came on, and then exercised with mom on the living room floor at night while reggae music blared from the stereo speakers. Then one day, almost miraculously, the pounds started shedding right before our eyes.

People started to notice my sudden shrinkage and began giving me complements. The difference with these compliments was that I actually believed them. When my mean violin teacher, Mr. Albright, called my name in orchestra practice, I was sure that I had done something wrong.

When I looked up from my instrument ready for the torment or complaint about my performance, he asked, "Madison, have you been losing weight?" "Yes," I answered timidly in utter surprise at what seemed to be a compliment from the most bitter man on the planet.

The first sign of weight loss was that these two funny looking bones emerged below my neck. Bones I don't ever remember seeing

The Ups and Downs of Being Round
Monica Marie Jones

or feeling on my body. Hallelujah, I had collarbones! As the pounds started to melt away the body of a woman started to surface, even though I was only 10 years old! As my middle shrunk, my 36 c's started to emerge. I had fully developed breasts before all of my other friends. They were so jealous. "You only have boobs because you used to be fat!" exclaimed my best friend Jaynelle. I didn't know whether to take it as a compliment or an insult. I was 10 years old with women's knockers (mom's favorite synonym for breasts; often used in reference to her favorite country singer, Dolly Parton) while all of my friends still sported My Little Pony and Care Bears training bras. I never had a use for one. How is it that you train a boob anyway?

My new life changing experience was very exciting but frightening at the same time. Things were happening so quickly. I was becoming a woman, while only in the fifth grade. I still wanted to rough house with the boys in the neighborhood and play with Barbie dolls with my girlfriends.

One morning I had a bad case of diarrhea. I hadn't had a mudslide like this since the laxative incident but I figured it was from the bean burrito that I had the night before. I was on the toilet all morning. When the Hershey squirt finally subsided I weakly walked to school. When I got home after school, I went in the bathroom to take a tinkle when I noticed a brown spot in my panties. I didn't want mom to think I had an accident, when she did the laundry so I called her to the bathroom.

"Ma, I had bad diarrhea this morning and didn't wipe my butt properly because there's a stain in my panties. I wanted to let you know, so you wouldn't think that I pooped my pants when you did the wash."

Mom inspected the stain and said, "Honey this isn't poop, this is dried blood, you've started your period." Before I could respond mom yelled to Ryan Jr, Auntie Lela and Grandma, "Our little girl is a woman now!"

Clearly embarrassed I yelled, "mom!" I was too late because she had already traipsed off to the living room to discuss my business further with my family. Why did this have to happen to me? I was only ten. I didn't want to be a woman yet. My new figure and my recent visit from Aunt Flow (blood flow that is) had opened new avenues that I didn't know existed.

In one last attempt to grasp my childhood, I decided that I would go to school without a bra on. Most of the girls my age were not wearing bras so what would be so wrong if I did the same? When I got to school things went along as usual, except one thing. The boys in class were talking to me more than usual. Just when I was beginning to enjoy all of the new attention, Mrs. Burnside called me up to her desk. Her desk was only 10 steps from my seat, but I took the long way around. As I approached her desk with a little extra hop in my step I noticed boy's heads turning one by one like dominoes falling in a row. When I finally arrived at her desk after my amateur gentlemen's club show, she motioned for me to come closer so that she could whisper what she had to tell me. When I came close she asked, "Do you own a bra?"

Embarrassed and well aware of the direction that this conversation was taking, I answered "yes."

The Ups and Downs of Being Round
Monica Marie Jones

"Well you need to start wearing it then," was her catty response. I walked back to my seat, taking the short cut and walking as still as I could as if I was balancing a book atop my head. I didn't want to draw any more attention to myself. After that day, I never went to school without a bra on.

As my physique continued to change, my half of a black girl booty also began to come to fruition. The other half was a white girl booty. My back continued on well past my hipbone, and plump, little curves that looked like the lower hook of the letter J completed the shape of the bottom where my butt met my hamstrings. So I guess you could say I had a J booty, straight and flat at the top and curved under at the bottom. It looked good in certain pants, but non-existent in others.

I could finally walk for miles without worrying about starting a fire in my inner thighs with my svelte, new figure. The years of rubbing had made it so that fabric that covered my inner thighs in all of my pants either had holes there or were worn to a sheer sheath of thread. Wearing a skirt without stockings or Daisy Duke styled shorts were out of the question, because the skin-on-skin friction would cause my inner thighs to be red and swollen. The only way to relieve myself of the inflammation was to walk like a cowboy with bowed legs.

All of the extra weight that I had carried around over the years made it so that my feet would lean over in my shoes causing the sides to scrape the ground and form holes there. I bid the control top pantyhose and girdles farewell. I no longer had to buy wide-width shoes. Sucking in my stomach was optional, no longer mandatory. I

The Ups and Downs of Being Round
Monica Marie Jones

could wear form-fitting clothes without looking "rolly poley" in them - even showing my mid-drift.

Things really started to change for me at school. Boys started to pay attention to me for my looks and not just my ability to get with the best of them in a game of pick 'em up mess 'em up (street tackle football). I thought that this might mean the end of the torturous teasing that I had endured over the years, but I thought too soon.

"White Girl!" she said. Well I guess it was better than "Miss Piggy," but Veronica just had to find something to say about me. I was fair skinned but most definitely NOT white. I don't know why I found it so insulting but I did. Perhaps I was upset by the mere fact had it came from Veronica's mouth and it was intended to hurt me. This time I did think of a quick comeback for the little greasy, black, zit faced, heifer that had tormented me over the years. "Black Girl!" I shouted back. Okay, maybe that wasn't so clever, but it was better. "Black and Beautiful!" she quickly retaliated. After glancing at the acne that had plagued her skin, probably due to her juicy jeri curl, a light bulb went off in my head, and I would issue my best comeback to date.

"Black and Bumpy!"

"Ha! Got her," I thought. All of the boys yelled "beast!" while the girls giggled. I got her back and she was quiet as her eyes began to dampen.

It was ironic, but I had obtained a little evil streak since I became slim and trim. I began to tease kids who I knew were weaker than me and would never retaliate. They didn't deserve it, but I had a lot of pent up aggression that I had to take it on someone. I made

The Ups and Downs of Being Round
Monica Marie Jones

others suffer as I had suffered all of those years. The only difference is that I would never tease people about their weight.

This newfound power that I felt as a thin person made me want to be that way forever. My worst fear was to be fat again. As far as I was concerned, my former fat self never existed. I made all of my best friends who knew me swear never to speak of my former weight again. I kept my past a secret from anyone I met from then on.

That year on Devil's Night, Jaynelle came knocking furiously at my door. "Maddy, let me in before I get picked up by the patty wagon!" Devil's night was the night before Halloween. In Detroit it was a big deal because people would set fires, commit crimes, and create all types of chaos around the city. In an effort to reduce the crime rate there was a citywide curfew for anyone under age eighteen starting at 6 p.m. If you were caught on the streets, you would be picked up by the "patty" wagon. The patty wagon was a big square vehicle that resembled a jail on wheels. They would pick up anyone caught committing crimes or youth who were violating the curfew. Arson was the major offense. Fires were often set to abandoned houses and dumpsters.

Jaynelle had come over to tell me that the dumpster behind my house had been set on fire. We cut through my backyard to the alley to check it out before the fire department got there. A few other kids from the neighborhood were feeding the fire with trash and sticks. I watched the roaring flames rise high then pop and crackle into sparks that resembled fireflies at the top. I felt the heat from the blaze and thought about how final fire was. When something was burned by fire it was gone forever. This made me think about my past.

The Ups and Downs of Being Round
Monica Marie Jones

    I ran back into the house and got a shoebox from under my bed. I quickly filled the shoebox with pictures and a few other tokens that reminded me of my fat days. Tonight, I would close the door on my past for good. I ran back outside and cast the box into the fire. I watched as the fire consumed and destroyed the remnants of my past.

    "What was that?" Jaynelle asked realizing that what I had thrown in was bigger than the small twigs and scraps of trash that everyone else had been tossing into the smoldering inferno. I didn't answer because I was entranced by the blaze. Just when I realized that Jaynelle was talking to me, we heard the screams of the police car and fire engine sirens coming. We simultaneously took off running to our homes.

Part Two:

Adolescence

"Phat Girl"

CHAPTER FOUR

Two Piece

I got a two-piece! No, not a two-piece with a biscuit from KFC, a two-piece swimming suit, and I looked good in it. It was lime green with black polka dots. Now that I was slim, I started dressing like a straight up hoochie. I finally had the figure I wanted and was going to flaunt it. Everyone from boys my age to old men the age of my grandfather were trying to get with me. To my surprise, everyone wasn't so happy about my recent weight loss. Some people were jealous.

"Fat girl," and "Miss Piggy" were replaced with "slut!" and "she thinks she's all that."

No, you *think* I'm all that, I *know,* I am all that. I received those negative comments from girls who were mad because I was getting attention from boys. If they really knew me, they wouldn't say those things.

The boys went from paying me no attention to offering comments like "hey baby" and "can a brother be down?"

I knew I was "all that" with my coral colored lipstick, fake sack chaser earrings from the beauty supply store, biker shorts with the neon green stripe down the side, and turquoise sports bra. Spandex and Lycra had always been my best friends because they were what fit me best. Stretchable clothing was my savior. But now they were even more of a treat because they accentuated every tantalizing curve of my new body.

The Ups and Downs of Being Round
Monica Marie Jones

I had also started doing my own hair. I would curl the right real tight with a small curling iron. It looked like I had an asymmetrical haircut. I did this because mom wouldn't let me cut my hair. I held the curling iron so tight, that my hair ended up breaking off and falling due to heat damage. I would have been better off cutting it. I was trying to live it up in my new body because I didn't know how long it would last. I thought I would make the best of it while it was there. I became what grown folks called "fast."

That Friday was the first hot day after the cruel Michigan winter that we had endured. Jaynelle and I decided to check out all the guys in their rides that we knew would be cruising down 7 Mile. We put on our biker shorts and sports bras then tried to tone it down a little with our "OPP" jackets, open of course. We were on our way to the penny candy store when a shiny royal blue Monte Carlo with flecks that sparkled like diamonds imbedded in the paint pulled up on the side of us. "Hey light skinneded girl!" Jaynelle's skin was the color of rich milk chocolate so deductive reasoning told me that he was referring to me. I turned around to see that the loud voice and bad grammar belonged to a guy that closely resembled one of the flying monkeys on the Wizard of Oz. I grimaced, sucked my teeth, and rolled my eyes all at the same time.

Just as I was about to discuss the degree of his ugliness with Jaynelle I heard him yell, "bump you then, trick! Don't nobody want to talk to your skank self no way!"

I was stunned to silence. Maybe being pretty and thin wasn't as fun as I thought it would be.

The Ups and Downs of Being Round
Monica Marie Jones

Since I had lived the best of both worlds (fat and skinny), I realized that people in general (the flying monkey and jealous girls excluded) are a whole lot nicer to you when you are skinny. What I mean is that nice people are nice to you whether you are fat or skinny, but they are almost too nice. For instance, two skinny girls will jokingly call each other fat, but won't jokingly call a fat person fat. Or people trying to be nice will subconsciously insult you by giving you a compliment like, "oh she has such a pretty face." Why couldn't they just say she is so pretty? Period. They might as well have said you've got a pretty face on that blubbery body of yours.

Friends would make jokes about other overweight people on TV or in the streets then catch themselves. They look over at you with an apologetic glance as if for the first time realizing that you too are plagued with that disgusting disease of being overweight. They look at you as if they are sorry, then say with their eyes, "oh, not you, you're not like that." Even worse is when your slender friend moans and complains about how fat she is. If she is fat, what does that make me? Obese? Thank God I didn't have to worry about that drama anymore.

Now that I was no longer rotund, people were generally nicer to me and I got things that I hadn't gotten before. Wasn't I the same person? Instead of white or economic privilege, I had slim privileges. Take dance class for instance. I worked at the same level of intensity that I had before. I could move a little better because I didn't have the excess booty baggage, but I was still pretty average. The dance studio director called my house one day and tells my mom that they want me to be a part of the company. The highest rank in the entire school!

The Ups and Downs of Being Round
Monica Marie Jones

"Are you sure?" she responded. Mom loved me but she knew that I wasn't all that when it came to dance, not yet anyway. I knew that it was mainly due to my new body. I had always had the pretty face, but now I had the body to match. I was now good enough to be in the company. I started getting asked to do more in the church, and at school. If I knew that I would get this special treatment for being thin, I would have been doing sit-ups, push ups, and chins ups on my umbilical chord before I popped out of the womb.

Dancing kept me in decent shape. Since I was already thin and getting regular exercise from dancing, I got lax on what I ate. I figured that like most other skinny people I could eat whatever I wanted and not worry about gaining weight. Dancing helped to increase my confidence. They thought I was good enough to be in the company, which made me think I was the stuff. When you think that you can do something, you usually do it well because you believe in yourself.

Despite the exercise I got from dancing, a few pounds crept back on as I got older. I didn't think much of it until people started calling me fat again. It started off with nicer descriptions like thick, shorty, thickums, big boned, healthy. Those were cool because I don't know too many black men who wanted a beanpole for a girlfriend. But when the fat comments and teasing started back up in the 8th grade, I thought what the heck are they talking about? Are they crazy? I looked good to myself in the mirror. I knew that every so often I would have to get a larger pant size but I really didn't shop that much so I didn't notice. And you know how you have clothes so long that they stretch to fit your body as your body grows? Well that is how it

The Ups and Downs of Being Round
Monica Marie Jones

was with me. I personally thought that I looked great. But no matter how good I thought I looked, someone would always think I was fat.

It was ironic. Women in particular think that they are fat no matter what size they are. They are never happy with themselves. I was satisfied with my size and thought I looked good. Anything was better than what I used to be. Even then, I didn't think anything was wrong with me until the cruel students at school were gracious enough to let me know. It was other people that led to my downfall. I would be fine with myself, and then people around me would make comments that would get me to thinking. Even if I were a twig, they would still find something to hate on me about.

CHAPTER FIVE

Security Measures

High School was a new beginning for me. I prayed that there would be no one that I knew from elementary school. I didn't need anyone knowing the secrets of my past. The guys were still sweating me, but I still received an occasional comment that would unnerve me. One guy asked Jaynelle, "Who's your friend? She's cute for a chubby girl." I was baffled. Where are they getting this from? I resolved to accept the term "thick" because I had never been skinny.

Skinny is the word commonly used as the opposite of fat and I knew that I was no longer fat. Did I have to be a size 2 to avoid the agony? I could fit into a size 8, okay maybe a 9/10, if I wanted to be comfortable, but either way, that was NOT fat.

It was all good though. I had several security mechanisms to measure my self worth. I used the attention that I got from guys as a barometer. I called it my Man-O-Meter. I used it as equally as I used the measurement of the hatred and jealousy that I received from the girls. I was still getting attention from the guys yet hate from the girls, so that confirmed to me that I had it going on. My sense of value was based on what others thought of me. It governed how I dressed, talked, wore my hair and how I felt about me. I no longer had any genuine sense of self. I wanted to be thin and well liked by others. I didn't do it for myself. In an attempt to stay fit and popular, I joined the dance club and the cheer team. This was yet another way to get attention from the guys.

The Ups and Downs of Being Round
Monica Marie Jones

My body issues also affected the type of man that I chose to date. I started dating in the 10th grade. Once I started dating, I typically leaned toward big guys because they made me feel safe and small. There was no worse feeling than being with a guy that was shorter, or weighed less than me. I didn't want to feel like if we got into some trouble on the streets, I would have to help him fight. I also didn't appreciate feeling that I could easily kick his butt. To be sure that this wasn't the case, I only gave guys who were six feet or taller and weighed well over two hundred pounds the time of day. They couldn't be sloppy. They had to be under control. I gravitated to athletic types - football players and wrestlers in particular.

During the second week of school, I was leaving my locker to go to civics class. On the way to class, I passed the football teams' lockers. I loved sashaying past their lockers and feeling their approving stares. Just as my runway show was about to end, I heard a husky voice call my name. I looked back and saw that the voice was that of Donte Houghton. I had been infatuated with him since we were in middle school together. He always had a girlfriend, so I admired him from afar.

"How do you know my name?" I asked.

"You went to Beaubien right?" he responded.

Oh my God, he actually remembered me.

"Yeah," I answered trying my best to sound unconcerned.

"Are you going to the sophomore swing out this weekend?"

I wasn't planning on it but I didn't want to seem like a lame.

"Yeah."

"Why don't you ride with me?"

The Ups and Downs of Being Round
Monica Marie Jones

I had never been on a date before, but couldn't let him know that. Will mom even say yes? What will I wear? How will I...

"Okay," I answered before he changed his mind or thought I was crazy for taking so long to respond.

"Cool, let me get your number so I can call you when I am on my way."

Shortly after that first date, we became an item. Everything seemed so perfect, and then one day things began to change. I was looking through his CD collection in his basement bachelor pad when I noticed him staring at me. I thought that he was admiring me when he burst my bubble by saying, "Baby, you need to stop visiting the cafeteria so much." Most of the other kids at our school used lunch as a social hour since they were done at 2:30 and could just go home and eat. I had to take advantage of my lunch hour because I stayed after school until 6pm for cheerleading and dance practice.

"Why do you say that?" I asked knowing full well where this conversation was headed.

"It's just that I want to keep you nice and tight like you were when I met you. I can't have you getting all big on me." He laughed. I'm glad he was able to find humor in this situation because I sure couldn't. I ignored him and continued perusing the CD's. I could no longer concentrate on the titles because I couldn't get his words out of my mind.

I felt the heat behind my eyes that was an all-too-familiar process - tears. I hated people seeing me cry. I put down the CD that I was looking at and crossed the room to go to the bathroom. Just as I

The Ups and Downs of Being Round
Monica Marie Jones

was about to cross Donte's path he reached out, poked his finger into my belly and said "hee hee!" like the chubby doughboy on the Pillsbury commercial. This cruel gesture triggered the teardrops that I had been struggling so hard to conceal. Normally I might have laughed the pain away or ignored something like this, but I was already riled up from his earlier comments.

I slapped his hand as hard as I could and took off running to the bathroom. I slammed the door with all of my might forgetting that I was not in my own home. The bathroom did not have a lock like at home, so I sat with my back against the door. I had my head down on my arms that were wrapped around my knees. I was attempting to halt my frantic sobbing when Donte plowed through the bathroom door. The shock of the force caused me to jerk my head up. When I did, my head met the door with a powerful blow.

Once he was completely in the bathroom he yelled, "What the heck is wrong with you? Your sensitive butt can't take a joke?"

"Jokes are supposed to be funny."

"Dang! I can't play with you? If anything I was trying to help you out."

"How is making fun of my weight supposed to help me out?"

"Look I never told you this, and I didn't think that I would have to, but I know that you used to be fat."

"What?" I whimpered.

"Before I went to Beaubien I went to Miller for a year in the third grade. You used to be friends with a girl named Sharla right?"

"Yeah," I said.

The Ups and Downs of Being Round
Monica Marie Jones

"Well she is my cousin. You don't remember me because I was only there for a year and I was real short and skinny. I didn't have a growth spurt until the summer after fifth grade. When I got to Beaubian, I knew that you looked familiar. Then I remembered that you were that little fat girl that used to hang out with Sharla. That's why I never spoke to you at Beaubian. Since you lost all that weight, I thought you were cute, but knew that you used to be fat and I didn't want to risk the chance that you might gain all that weight back. When I saw you once we got in high school, I figured if you had kept it off this long that you could probably keep it off for good, so I gave it a shot. But lately you have been gaining a few pounds and I don't want you going back to your old ways. What I am trying to say is, you have the potential to be fat. And I aint trying to be seen with no fat girl."

Dang! I tried to keep my past a secret and this is exactly why. I knew that people would hold it against me. Of all of the people that had to find out, why him? His cruel words paralyzed me. His last sentence, "I aint trying to be seen with no fat girl," was etched in my brain.

I called Jaynelle when I got home and told her the whole story.

"Girl, forget him! You need to dump his behind," she said immediately following the end of my story.

"But maybe he's right. Maybe I do need to lose some weight." I said weakly.

"Yeah maybe you do. You need to lose him because he's nothing but dead weight."

The Ups and Downs of Being Round
Monica Marie Jones

Jay always took my side no matter what, even if I was wrong. I just wanted her to tell it like it was. Like Donte had.

"Come on Jay, you know that I could stand to loose a few pounds. I am not as skinny as I used to be."

"So what? You are smart, beautiful, talented and popular. What more could a guy ask for? If I were your boyfriend, I would be going around bragging, 'do ya'll know Madison Jenson?' and they would say, 'you mean the pretty girl that's a cheerleader and in the dance club?' and I would be like 'yeah, that's *MY* woman.'"

"Girl, shut up! I am not anything to be bragging about." Although I do have to admit that she was making me feel a whole lot better. Jaynelle was always good at doing that.

Beep!

"Hold on girl."

"Hello."

"Who are you on the phone with?" Donte asked possessively.

"Hold on Donte." I clicked back over.

"Jaynelle, I'll call you right back okay?"

"I hope you not getting off the phone with me for Donte's sorry...." I cut her off and clicked back over before she could finish.

"Hello..."

"Naw, don't get off of the other line on my account, you must be talking to one of your little boyfriends."

This fool was a trip. One minute he is dogging me out and the next minute he is trying to act jealous. I can't lie and say that I wasn't flattered, because it showed me that he cared. Before I could open my mouth to respond all I heard was...

The Ups and Downs of Being Round
Monica Marie Jones

Click!

I figured I would let him calm down a bit before I talked to him and I called Jaynelle back.

"Yeah girl, that was him, trying to act all jealous."

"Yeah right, possessive is more like it. He's always trying to keep tabs on you. It's a control thing."

"I just take it as his way of showing that he cares."

"I'm for real. Now, like I was saying before, if he can't appreciate what he's got, then he needs to get to step."

She was right, but like a dummy I stayed with him anyway. Donte is very handsome and popular. I was glad that he wanted to be with someone like me. So I took his verbal abuse. I felt that as long as he wasn't putting his hands on me, it was OK. The devastating bathroom incident would not be the last time Donte made comments about my weight. None of it hurt as bad as that particular incident. However another incident did come close.

One day he was making sarcastic remarks about my weight. Normally I would ignore his comments or laugh them off, but this time I decided to respond.

I said, "You were so nice to me at the beginning of our relationship. You used to shower me with compliments. What happened?"

He said, "That was all a part of the chase, I got you now." In other words, now that he got what he wanted, he no longer needed to go out of his way to be nice. I felt like that toy that you wanted for Christmas. Once you got it and played with it for a while, exciting.

The Ups and Downs of Being Round
Monica Marie Jones

To the outside world we looked like a happy and perfect couple. We won class couple for the mock elections in the senior yearbook. By that year, I made captain of the cheerleading team and the dance club. Even though I had put on a few extra pounds, being with me was as good for Donte's reputation as being with him was good for my feelings of self worth.

As graduation neared, I had decided to attend Eastern Michigan University. I chose Eastern because it was the best school for me since I wanted to become a teacher. It was not too far from home, yet not too close. Jaynelle decided to pass on college when her uncle got her a good paying job at the plant. I was sad because in elementary school we made a pact that we would go to all the same schools together all the way through college. We had done so thus far, until college. Donte was offered a football scholarship to the University of Minnesota and decided to attend there.

On prom night we stayed up late and talked about our futures. He started the conversation by saying, Do you think that we will last in a long distance relationship?"

"I don't mind trying if you don't mind trying," I said trying not to sound too eager about either decision, knowing full well that I wanted us to stay together.

"Well, it's just that it might be hard with us being so far apart."

"I think that we can make it work if we really want to," I said not trying to sound too pathetic.

"Well, don't be down there messing around with other dudes on me," he said. I was surprised that he gave a care.

The Ups and Downs of Being Round
Monica Marie Jones

"And you don't be down there messing with other chicks. You know they're going to be on your jock because you play football," I said jokingly, yet serious as a heart attack.

"All right then baby, we'll give it a try."

Graduation was a week later. I was so happy to be getting out of school that I didn't know what to do with myself. Along with graduating from high school, I had also graduated from dance, cheerleading, and being thin. I was officially considered thick. This wasn't a bad thing because many guys preferred women with a little meat on their bones. Since high school hadn't turned out to be the fresh start that I thought it would be, I was really looking forward to going off to college.

No one there would know that I used to be fat. I could hide my body issues and personal insecurities.

Part Three:

College

"The Freshman Fifteen"

CHAPTER FIVE

Freshman fifteen…sophomore fifteen…junior fifteen…

They say when you get to college, you gain the notorious freshman fifteen, but they didn't say that you would keep on gaining and gaining and gaining…When I got to college, dance wasn't as readily available as it was in high school, so I no longer had that outlet for maintaining my weight. Collegiate cheerleading was on a whole different level than high school. It was like a sport and they were good at it. There were also guy cheerleaders who picked the girls up and tossed them around like they rag dolls. I was up to 160 pounds, so there was no way they could toss me around so easily.

They did have a dance squad but their tops were tight and cut below the nipple. Their pants were also tight. They had broken thick girl rule number one - that there must be opposition in the fit of your top and your bottom. This means that you can wear a tight top if you have on loose pants, you can wear tight pants if you have on a loose top, and you can wear loose pants and a loose top. Wearing a tight top and tight pants at the same time, especially if there is space between the two was a definite NO-NO. Either way, it leads to a disastrous avalanche of flab over the top of your pants, or there is the central squeeze which is caused by the simultaneous pressure coming from both directions of the tight top and bottom which will cause your mid section to balloon out to look like an inner tube. I wasn't as firm as I used to be so I didn't feel comfortable enough to try out because if I did make it, I had no intention of wearing the uniform.

I was looking forward to my membership to the university's gym that was included in our tuition. If I worked out really hard, I could lose some weight for Donte. I wouldn't see him until Christmas break which was four months away. That would be plenty of time to lose a good twenty pounds. He would be so happy if I got my body back to the way it used to be. I soon learned that losing the weight would not be as easy as I thought.

The university had a gym, but all of the working out didn't mean a thing if you continued to eat the fat and calorie laden foods that the school offered. You would think that an establishment of higher learning might have figured proper nutrition into the equation, but I guess not. On top of that, they gave us a meal card with an allowance of over $300 a month. If we didn't spend it all it didn't carry over, so we felt obligated to spend it. I was not going to let money or food go to waste, so I made sure to spend it all every month. One month I managed to spend it all a week before the month was over. I'm not sure how I did that but I was scared I might have to fast for that last week. Fortunately my friends helped by buying me a meal here and there so I made it through.

New beginnings and endings

College life was a major change in lifestyle for me. The separation from home, my boyfriend, and all things that I had become accustomed to triggered the beginning of my slow decline, or should I say increase? An increase in weight that is. The first thing that I had to get accustomed to was my new roommate, Katrina. She was short,

The Ups and Downs of Being Round
Monica Marie Jones

sickeningly cute, charismatic and had a wonderful personality. You couldn't hate her for how cute she was. We clicked immediately and did everything together. I enjoyed her company. The only thing that was really hard getting accustomed to was being the underdog.

Wherever we went, I looked like chopped liver next to her. She was cute and had a great body to match. She was came to school on a track scholarship, so she was fit. Sometimes when we would go out together, guys would approach me and I would get excited, until I found out that they were coming my way to ask me to hook them up with her. Sometimes I would be nice and relay the message. If I was in a funky mood, I would either say, "okay," and never tell her, or I would blurt out some rude response like, "tell her yourself!"

I knew that I was wrong, but I was tired of that scenario. I wanted guys to come to me for me, not because they were trying to approach my girl! It wasn't bad at first because I reminded myself that I had a boyfriend. But after a while, that didn't work because the calls and letters from Donte became few and far between.

I could hear the lack of interest in his voice the few times we did talk. I was always good at detecting when trouble was on the way. You would think that that characteristic would be like a gift, but it felt like a curse. Sometimes I wished I were an airhead so that I would be oblivious to the inevitable. After all, ignorance is bliss.

Donte and I broke up shortly after the first semester of my freshman year began. He was living it up in Minnesota and was the only freshman on his team that was good enough to be on the starting line up, which brought a slew of athlete groupies his way. I soon realized that he was too young to be tied down, especially in a long

The Ups and Downs of Being Round
Monica Marie Jones

distance relationship. Or at least that was what he said. The truth was probably that he figured, why stay with one girl who has the potential to be fat when he could have all of the hot women that he wanted. After three weeks of not hearing from him I got an email. It read:

Hey Maddy,

I am meeting a lot of new people out here and it has made me realize that I am too young to be in such a serious relationship. Especially with it being long distance and all. You know you are my girl so we can always be friends but I think it would be best if we went our separate ways.

Peace.

Donte

So just like that it was over. I had been dumped through an email by a frigging email. He couldn't tell me face to face because of the distance, but he didn't even have the decency to tell me over the phone. I wasn't fazed by his weak break up because of I had been distracted by all of the fine men on my campus.

CHAPTER SIX

A Night Out on the Town While Being Round

My man-o-meter was in full effect because when I wasn't hanging with Katrina, I was getting attention from the guys on campus. I felt I still had it going on, but something was different. I was turning heads here and there but was not getting the volume of head turning that I was used to.

I noticed that smaller girls, attractive or not, were getting more attention than me. I felt ignored. There were times when guys didn't even acknowledge my existence. I was used to ignoring all the attention that I was getting because there was just too much. Now guys walked past me as if I wasn't there. This was not cool. I had to do something. For years, this is how I had measured my worth. If I did not have the praise of men, what did I have left? To make matters worse, girls were nice to me. The sideways stares or looks of intimidation were not shot my way anymore. I was no longer a threat to them. Up to this point in my life, I had survived by letting the judgment of others determine my self-worth. How could I survive like this?

I did anything I could to get attention. I first tried using what I had, which was a decent rack, so I would wear push up bras and shirts with plunging necklines. I also knew that I could dance in an exotic way that would turn heads, so I went to all the parties and clubs and

The Ups and Downs of Being Round
Monica Marie Jones

grinded my way on the dance floor. It turned heads and made men's imaginations wander. I could read their minds through their eyes.

"If she can move like that on the dance floor, no telling what she can do in the bedroom." That's what they were thinking. I didn't intend to attract that kind of attention, but something was better than nothing.

One Saturday night we decided to go clubbing back at home in Detroit. I went with Katrina, Jaynelle, and two other girls. One of the girls was Katrina's cousin Shantiece. She was the color of cappuccino with extra cream. She had long dark brown hair and a nice body. Her waist was small and she had the proper apportion of hips, butt and chest. She also had a certain swagger when she walked. Jaynelle and our girl Cordette from high school met us there. Cordette was light, bright, and almost white. She had the type of hair that she could wash, blow dry and flat iron and it would look like a silky straight fresh perm. She could just wet her hair and it would curl up. She had what some people call "good hair." But does that mean that all of the black people that weren't blessed with those types of tresses have bad hair? I think not. My dad had that kind of hair, but unfortunately those traits were not passed on to me.

Cordette was quite the airhead. Having once been the slim, pretty girl taught me that you can't turn your head every time a guy calls out to get your attention. Sometimes ignoring them is the best way to go. Anytime I went somewhere with Cordette she would respond to every single call, whistle, or "DAAANNNNG!" that came out of a guy's mouth. She would swing her head around and say, "huh?" I personally think that the head swing was just to get some

The Ups and Downs of Being Round
Monica Marie Jones

whip action going with her hair; to make sure people noticed it. It was nauseating. She was so nice that I couldn't bring myself to hate her. I envied how clueless she was because she never noticed any negative attention that was directed to her. My keen sense of awareness made it rare for me to miss any of the negative energy that was directed towards me.

Everyone had on skimpy, sexy outfits. Everyone except for me. I wore stretch jeans and a loose fitting v-neck cotton shirt from Express. It was meant to be a close fitting shirt but I purposefully bought it one size too big so it wouldn't cling to the rolls that had formed on my back. Jaynelle must have been making some good money at the plant because she was looking fabulous. She was the same size that she was in high school. She was even a little more toned from the industrial labor that she had to do at work. She had on a sexy, expensive, name brand outfit with some boots to match. Her hair was freshly cut and styled and her neck ears, wrists, and ankles were adorned with gold and diamonds. I had almost felt like she had overdone it before I remembered that that was how they did it in Detroit, really flashy.

It was empty when we first got to the club. We came early on purpose to avoid the inflated cover charge. We walked around the place, got our drinks while we waited for the club to fill up. Within the next hour, I was wishing we could go back in time to the club's less crowded moments. It was packed and hot. As we made our way though the crowd trying to avoid separation, I noticed all of the heads my friends were turning. A guy grabbed Jaynelle's hand to bring her closer so that he could talk to her. A tall light skinned guy with a velour jogging outfit asked Cordette to dance. Katrina wandered off to the bar with an older man that looked like a sugar daddy who wanted to buy her a drink. He had a pimped out hat with a feather in it. As I continued to make my way through the crowd all eyes were on Shantiece. It was just a matter of who she wanted to give the time of day. Finally a fine caramel brother with a fat diamond earring in each ear caught her eye and they walked off to a booth in a dark corner to get to know each other better.

    As far as I could tell, not one man looked my way. I went out to the dance floor and did a basic two-step to the beat. I didn't want to sweat my hair out and I didn't want to draw the wrong attention by dancing too freaky. I sucked on each piece of ice from my cup hoping that maybe some guy would find my ice-sucking sexy and approach me. When I swallowed the last drop of ice I realized that that the idea had failed miserably.

    The dance floor started to fill up and not one guy had asked me to dance all night. I tried to do a few exotic dance moves, but no one paid attention. Soon I started getting brushed and bumped by all types of butts and breasts on top of catching a few swift elbows here and there. I was in the way of all of the sweaty grinding couples out there so I just decided to leave the dance floor. I found a small circular table in a dark corner and sat there for the rest of the night. I watched my friends having a great time and started to feel jealous. Why didn't anyone want to give me the time of day? I felt that dreaded stinging behind my eyes and had to do everything in my power to fight the tears back. If anyone asked me why my eyes were red, I would just say that the smoke was getting to me.

The Ups and Downs of Being Round
Monica Marie Jones

    I felt invisible. During my childhood I wanted to be invisible so that the other kids would stop teasing me. When I lost weight, I became visible and loved it. Now, I was invisible again hated it. I wanted to catch the attention of young, appealing men that were in my peer group. Nasty old men and ugly lame guys didn't count.

    At 2:00 a.m. the lights came on to let everyone know that it was time to go. Most of the people lingered to exchange numbers and talk for just a few more minutes with the person that they met that night. Pens and pencils were no longer necessary tools for this process. Everyone was whipping out cell phones to save those precious digits in the phone's memory. When my girls were finally done they came over and Jaynelle said, "Girl, we have been looking for you. Are you ready?" Did it look like I was busy with anything besides twiddling my thumbs? "Yeah girl, I'm ready." Shantiece was still all hugged up with the fine guy with the earrings. I guess that he was going to walk her to the car.

    The exit was narrow so we all plowed out single file. Katrina led the line then Cordette and Jaynelle followed. Shantiece and her pretty boy were in front of me. Just before we got to the door Shantiece's new boy toy reached his long arm out and opened the door for our line. He let Katrina, Cordette, Jaynell and Shantiece through. Just when I was about to step through, he stepped in front of me and went through dropping the door on me. I would have been shocked or appalled if this were the first time that this had occurred, but lately this was a regular practice. Since I was the biggest of all of my friends, he figured that I would be strong enough to handle the weight of the door on my own. Maybe since they were so small, they were too delicate and fragile to be strong enough to open the door on their own. This incident was the perfect way to end my horrible night. It was typical with everything else that had occurred. No one looked at me, no one asked me to dance or offered to buy me a drink and I got a door dropped on me.

On a Mission to get attention

The next day I was back to thinking of ways that I could get more attention. I didn't want to go through any more nights like last night. That week at school I paid more attention to everything that went on. I noticed that the girls that got the most attention on campus were in sororities. I also remembered that all of the girls who were on line last semester had lost a lot of weight by the time that they crossed. That was an added incentive for me. I decided to pledge.

I went to all of the campus functions and community events but they were really for girls who were interested in membership. I attended every program and kissed butt. The brown nosing coupled with my grades and campus involvement made me an excellent candidate.

When I found out that I was chosen to be on line, I was ecstatic. I now had a chance at being noticed by the guys. I was determined to be the best pledge that there was. When I got on line, they immediately recognized that my weight was an issue for me. They knew that it was my weakness, and played on that weakness knowing that it was the only way that they could get to me. When they told me that my line name would be Miss Piggy, I quit on the spot. All of my attempts to get attention had failed and my self-esteem began to plummet.

The Ups and Downs of Being Round
Monica Marie Jones

The quality of guys was interested in me declined as well. On Friday night, I decided to go to a house party with Katrina. She was dating one of the guys who lived there and asked me to join her. I didn't have anything else planned so I tagged along. The party was pretty lame. There were five guys and five girls there so it ended up being a hook up party. The guy that decided to attach himself to me was a homely freshman named Boris. His name alone turned me off, but to make matters worse he was shaped like Grimace, the big purple McDonalds creature. I could never figure out what species of animal Grimace was. Boris had a cute face, was over six feet tall, 300 pounds. Aside from the cute face, he was far from the men that I envisioned to fit into my manly mold. He was passive, yet all on my jock. I liked a little bit of a challenge when it came to the men that I dated. A little cockiness and arrogance also turned me on. I was caught up in my thoughts when I realized that I was being awfully picky. I had my nerve. I wasn't all that or else more guys would have been paying me more attention. I should be glad that anyone was interested in me at all, I reasoned. I could very well be sitting here by myself while everyone else was all coupled up. So I decided to humor him since everyone else was hooked up and Katrina did not look like she would be ready to leave anytime soon.

I was annoyed by his presence at first but then something strange happened. He began to shower me with compliments. He told me how beautiful I was and that he couldn't believe that he was here with such a gorgeous girl. It felt great because I couldn't even remember the last time that anyone had placed me on such a pedestal.

He put the icing on the cake by saying that he felt like he was in a dream that had come true.

It had been so long since I had received flattery from a man. I had been rejected by guys so much that it felt good to have someone want me. It was all a part of my, "I can't be alone syndrome." I always had to have someone want me to feel good about myself - I always had to have a boyfriend, a love interest, or something of that nature on hand. That night I was able to look past Boris' uninviting appearance and passive demeanor. While everyone at the party made merry until the morning light, I slept on the futon in his arms, as he laid awake watching me and showering me with compliments and planting soft, gentle kisses on my forehead.

Fat with Family

My encounter with Boris happened on the Friday night before Christmas break. On Sunday I went home to spend the holidays with my family. I was glad to be home and happy to see everyone after being away at school. I wore my favorite tight, brown flared pants and my cream and brown fitted turtle neck to match. I thought that I was looking pretty good. I had seen a few people from high school while I was out shopping at the mall. Several of the girls that I had graduated with had really blown up and looked more like old aunties than young college students. That made me feel better because at least I didn't look as bad as they did. I was walking out of the kitchen feeling glad to have a home cooked meal when my cousin Sharon said, "I guess they've been feeding you well up at school, cause you done packed on some pounds." I rolled my eyes as hard as I could without them falling out and stormed back into the kitchen. I thought that my family

The Ups and Downs of Being Round
Monica Marie Jones

would be a safe haven where I would not have to deal with the day-to-day reminders of my weight, but I was mistaken.

CHAPTER SEVEN

Happy New Year?

When I got back to school in January I made an attempt to get active again. Losing weight had been my number one resolution the last four years. I had never been able to keep it past February, but I was trying once again. I was searching the kiosk at school in hopes of finding a spinning or aerobics class when I came across a flyer that caught my eye. It was for a hip hop dance workshop. A famous choreographer from New York was visiting the university to teach a master class sponsored by the dance department. I called the number on the flyer and registered. When I got there I realized that although it was a hip-hop class, I was the only black person there besides the instructor. I took a spot front and center.

I knew that I had skills, so perhaps this choreographer would discover me and want to take me back to New York to dance with his company. I danced harder than I had ever danced before. I felt tired and winded because I hadn't danced in so long but I tried my best not to let it show. I could hear the "oohs" and "aahs" coming from some of the students behind me, which motivated me to dance harder. After warming us up and teaching us random movements, he went through a combination that was high energy and intense. I am a fast learner so I caught on quickly and began helping others. At the end, he had us perform it in five groups of five. I practiced the dance in the back with each and every group. I was always taught never to sit down in dance class.

When the five groups were done performing we formed a cipher where each person got to showcase their individual talents. I did a Broadway slide into the circle then transitioned into a pas de burree, which was my prep for a double pirouette. I know that it was a hip-hop class, but I thought that I would give them a little taste of my ten years of formal dance training. I finished with an impromptu hip-hop combination showcasing my knowledge of all of the latest moves. The close of my performance was met with raucous applause from the other dancers.

When it was over, I was dripped with sweat and was gasping for air. That's when I saw the choreographer coming my way. As he approached, I did my best to gather my composure. I sucked my stomach in and stood up straight.

When he got close to me he said, "Hey sweetheart, what is your name?" "Maddy," I answered, trying to mask the fact that I didn't have the breath to get more than the first two syllables of my name out of my mouth. I figured that Maddy would make a good stage name for a famous dancer in New York. "You are really an excellent dancer," Just when I was getting my hopes up, my dreams were shattered when he continued by saying, "You know I have a friend that is about your size. You remind me of her. She can dance really well, just like you, but she just doesn't have the confidence to perform because she is so self conscious about being overweight."

Why couldn't he have just said I was an excellent dancer and left it at that? Did he really have to go on to tell me the story about his pitifully fat friend who was just like me? Don't people know that a compliment followed by a fat comment is worse than an insult or no compliment at all? I responded with a weak, "Thank you," and a fake smile before I grabbed my dance bag and exited the studio. So much for being discovered and becoming a famous New York dancer, I thought.

A chance at love?

Despite my decline in attention from the fellas (except for the likes of Boris), my dancing dis from the New York choreographer, and Sharon's observation of my extra bulge, I still had a great college experience. Katrina and I found every possible reason to throw a party at our new apartment. We would party until the sun came up. On top of birthdays, holidays, and weekends, we concocted several other party themes. Thirsty Thursdays were the parties where we got our drink on because most students didn't have Friday classes. Chicken Wangz and Thangz happened when I was in the mood to fry up a slew of my famous fried chicken wing dings accompanied by my version of Red Lobster's famous cheddar and garlic biscuits made from scratch. We also hosted the after party for any event that happened on campus. These events were everything from talent shows to date auctions. Whatever the occasion, there was an abundance of food and drink.

Both of our birthdays were in March so we had a joint birthday bash. The night was great! Just when I thought it was too late for any more guests to arrive, in walked a group of five guys, but I only noticed one. His smile was so beautiful that it made me oblivious to

The Ups and Downs of Being Round
Monica Marie Jones

the other four who had entered before. Beyond his smile, I was enamored by the fact that he fit my manly mold-perfectly. If I had to give the complexion of his skin a title, the only fit name would have been toasted almond honey drop. He was at least 6'4 and well over two hundred pounds. He may have been close to 300, but it looked good on him. He seemed taller because he carried himself so well, his head held high in confidence. From the look of his build, it was clear that he had played or was currently playing some sport or worked out regularly. He was big and solid. He could probably wrap those strong arms and large hands around me one and a half times if he squeezed hard enough. Twice would have been pushing it. At this point I was nowhere near the thin and firm girl that I used to be. I was borderline fat. I wasn't so big that I still did not turn heads but 20 to 30 more pounds could have made me completely invisible to the opposite sex, which almost seems paradoxical because people could not miss such a huge tub of lard.

That night I laid it on thick and ended up getting his attention. His name was Davin but his friends called him *"D"* for short. I joined them at the table for a game of spades and flirtatiously called him *D* as if I had known him all of my life. We were on a team together. I made sure that it ended up that way. I would tried to sound sexy, "it's your turn D," or if he made a book I said, "you go D!"

I must have sounded desperate. Normally, I was never one to flirt, but there was something about him that pushed me past my regular limits. He was probably thinking, "do I know this girl? Why is she calling me D like we go way back or something?"

The Ups and Downs of Being Round
Monica Marie Jones

I was not the only one trying to get his attention. A few of the other girls at the party were batting their eyelids and giggling at all of his jokes. He wasn't fazed by any of us. I tried to get more information about him from Katrina, but she didn't know who he was. It turns out that one of his boys had a class with Katrina and she invited him to come to the party. Throughout the night, several girls tried to sway him in their direction. As usual all of those girls were thin and cute. I figured that I didn't have much of a chance against them so I just gave up and went about my business getting my party on and playing the hostess role.

Later that night I was sipping on some lemonade while doing the hustle with some of my girls. I was feeling tired so I sat down on the couch and closed my eyes for a minute. I opened my eyes when I felt a tap on my shoulder. I looked up and it was Davin sitting on the arm of the couch.

"You okay?" He asked

"Yeah, I'm cool." I responded wondering why he even cared. I looked around the room and noticed that the other girls that were trying to pursue him had looks of defeat on their faces as they glared in our direction.

"So this is your party, huh?" He asked trying to spark up a conversation.

"Yeah, well, me and my roommate. We both have birthdays this month."

"Oh yeah? Happy Birthday! How old are you?" He asked reaching for his wallet.

The Ups and Downs of Being Round
Monica Marie Jones

"I'm 22..." I was about to ask him how old he was just to keep the conversation going. That's when he pulled out a crisp twenty and two ones and pinned them to the measly stack of six-dollar bills that I already had pinned above my right breast. I shuddered when I felt his knuckle brush the skin of my chest as he secured the money with the pin in place. I tried my best to stop from shivering. It took all of the energy that I had to do that so I didn't have any left to speak. He said, "Would it be possible for me to give you a call sometime? Maybe I can take you out for your birthday."

I tried my best not to sound too eager and responded with a cool, "Sure." When we exchanged numbers those other girls were seething. I just know that they were wondering what in the world he would want with a thick girl like me when he could have had any of them. It turns out that to my advantage he has a preference for thick women. For once I was not the one looking on in awe. I got the guy! The feeling was unexplainable. That night I played the scene over and over in my head before I fell fast asleep.

Davin called me three days later. When I saw his name come up on the caller ID I had to gather my composure, so I let it ring twice so as not too appear too eager. We talked for three hours going over all of the basic get to know you stuff. Then he asked me if I had any plans for dinner. We decided to go to a Cajun restaurant in Ann Arbor. When we got there, I was trying my best to eat and act like a lady. Every few minutes I would brush my tongue over my teeth to make sure there weren't any unsightly gobs of food stuck there. To keep the conversation going I asked, "So what made you ask for my

The Ups and Downs of Being Round
Monica Marie Jones

number out of all of the girls who were on your tip at the party?" I had been dying to know.

"Well first of all, I thought that you were pretty, but what really caught my attention was that you were not sweating me like they were. I mean you were friendly but you didn't throw yourself on me. You also didn't expect me to be interested in you." He had obviously mistaken my feelings of inadequacy for confidence.

"Well I don't know if you noticed or not but I was kind of flirting with you when we were playing cards."

"I didn't notice, I thought that you were just enjoying the game. But once the game was over you just went on about your business. You weren't hounding me or trying to be all up in my face. Sometimes girls will do anything to get a guys attention, and they think that we are too stupid to realize what they are trying to do."

Thank God I hadn't tried any of my attention getting tactics on him.

"You gave me somewhat of a challenge. I had to come over and pursue you. Believe it or not guys don't always want everything handed to them on a platter. Sometimes they like to work for what they really want."

Oh my goodness! He really wants *ME*? At that moment I felt so validated. But this time was different. It wasn't like in the past when I used how good a guy thought I looked to measure my worth. This time I felt respected as a person too.

After dating for a few months, one night we were getting ready to go play laser tag. He watched me as I was in the bathroom mirror applying eyeliner when he asked, "Why do you wear make-up?"

The Ups and Downs of Being Round
Monica Marie Jones

Baffled and caught off guard by his question I asked. "What do you mean?" His response was, "You look beautiful without it. You have natural beauty." I was floored. All of these years I was sure that I needed to wear make-up, fancy clothes, sweet hair do's and be lean to be beautiful. He turned my world upside down because here he was telling me I was beautiful without make-up. Others of a similar nature followed this compliment, but it was what he didn't do that affected me the most. Never once did he criticize me about my weight as my boyfriends had done in the past. This bewildered me because we went out to dinner and cooked for each other so much that I had put on a whopping 30 pounds since we met. Could a man really love me just as I was?

CHAPTER EIGHT

Crash diet

That summer Katrina and I decided to plan a trip to the Caribbana. I had visited this Caribbean festival in Toronto with my family in years past but I had never gone as an adult. It was three months away and I decided that I would go on a diet right quick to try to get cute so I could wear sexy outfits. When I was in the gym at school, I came across an announcement on the bulletin board about a weight loss study. "GET PAID TO LOSE WEIGHT!" was plastered across the top of the sheet in bold letters. They wanted to test some new diet pill before putting it out on the market. They also put you on a meal and exercise plan. I figure I had nothing to lose, but some unwanted weight, so I called the number and signed up as soon as I got home.

For the next eight weeks I had to walk a mile a day 4 times a week and record everything that I ate. I also had to take these big brown stinky horse pills that they gave me twice a day. Half of the group had the placebo and the other half had the real thing. I knew that I had the real thing because as soon as I popped the first one I was bouncing off of the walls. We had to turn in our meal sheets every week, but I only recorded what I thought they might approve of. When I slipped up and ate junk, I would keep it as my little secret. I would pop an extra pill that day to make up for it. I also decided not to share the fact that I was participating in this study with Katrina or

The Ups and Downs of Being Round
Monica Marie Jones

Davin. I didn't want them to think I was some big fat loser who could only lose weight by taking drugs and getting paid for it.

When the study was done, I had lost twenty pounds. Whenever someone asked me how I did it I lied and said, "I ate right and I exercised." I was able to buy some really cute outfits for the trip and I even bought a two-piece. I wasn't going to push it by getting a string bikini, but I got a tankini. The top was like a tank top and the bottom was like a pair of boy shorts, or hot pants according to my mom. I had seen women that were twice my size wearing bikinis proudly, so why not give it a try? When we got home from the mall I modeled all of my new items for Katrina. I saved my bathing suit for last and pranced out like I was a famous diva. Katrina had a genuine look of awe in her face when she said, "I wish I was as confident as you."

This statement took me by surprise coming out of Katrina's mouth. I always thought Katrina to be confident and beautiful. She was not skinny, but she was petite and had flesh in all of the right places. She had a small waist, shapely hips, and boobs that were not too big or too small. She had a layer of soft flesh over her stomach, but it was appealing, not unpleasant. Just by looking at her I could tell she was at least fifty pounds lighter than I was. She was no longer running track but her body was still beautiful. She was shaped like a pear, while I on the other hand was beginning to slowly resemble the shape of an eggplant. The truth was that I had always been envious of her self-assurance. She had her own style and could dress to kill. She had no problem kicking it with guys and she had lots of friends. I wanted to tell her this and let her know that the confidence that I was exuding was merely a show for others and an effort to convince myself.

"Why do you say that Kat? I think that you are very confident."

"Well I would never have the confidence to wear a two piece as proudly as you are wearing that one."

"Girl, you would probably look better because you weigh less than me."

"It doesn't make a difference either way because the guys always look at the light skinned girl with the long hair first. By the time their done using all their energy on them, they don't have the time to acknowledge my existence."

I was stunned. I never knew that Kat felt this way. I thought that her smooth mocha complexion and her short sleek coif were two of her best attributes. And unless I had imagined it all, I remember guys sweating her since the day that we met.

"Kat, I may be light skinned, and have my fair share of hair, but if I do get the honor of being looked at, it's not until after all of the thin girls are looked at first. It doesn't matter if they are light, dark, ugly, or bald as an eagle." I knew from experience that being the chubby girl in the group was far worse than being the dark skinned girl in the group. Or at least that was what I thought.

"Maddy, you can loose weight, you have already proved that, but unless I wake up as Michael Jackson, I cannot change my skin color."

After that I didn't know what else to say. She was right. I could change my situation. I felt selfish because there are so many

The Ups and Downs of Being Round
Monica Marie Jones

people who have situations for which change is beyond their control. If they had the power they would do anything to change their circumstances. I had the power but for some reason, I just couldn't tap into it.

I was so busy partying at Caribbana and celebrating the weight I'd lost that I had stopped eating right and exercising cold turkey. It didn't help that Caribbean men actually like their women with a little meat on their bones. I drank twice as much as I normally did and ate whatever I desired whenever I wanted. I ended up gaining the twenty pounds back almost as quickly as I had lost them, plus an additional ten.

The 30 pounds that I had gained weren't as bad as I thought they would be. My years of dancing and my occasional visits to the gym had made it so that I had quite a bit of muscle tone. I read a book that said that muscle weighs more than fat. I also found that people who said that they weighed less than me often looked much more stout than I did. Muscle or not I was still fairly huge. I noticed mainly when I looked at pictures of myself and when my clothes started getting too tight. All of the torments of my past slowly came back to haunt me. The inner thigh rub, and control top panty hose were among the first to resurface. There was a new thing added to the list this time…the boob quartet.

The boob quartet occurs when your bra gets too small or your boobs have gotten too big, whichever way you choose to perceive it. It looks like you have four boobs because the top of your bra forms a division in the middle of each breast. Your two new breasts are formed from the spillage of your old breasts over the top of that dividing line. My breasts were no longer the center point of attention on my body like they had been in the past. They now were in constant competition with my stomach to see which could stick out the farthest.

I was what you might call borderline big, which I personally think is the worst big of all. I wasn't so fat that people felt sorry for me or felt bad talking about me. I felt like I caught all of the heat for all of the people my size and larger because they thought I could handle it. I wasn't so far gone that there seemed to be no hope. I was just far enough to be criticized, ridiculed, and looked down upon as having no will power.

What people didn't understand was that I used to be in shape and that made it harder for me to lose weight. I always had to step it up a notch to see results. If I was four hundred pounds and bed ridden, I might burn hundreds of calories by just getting up and walking from the bedroom to the living room. A person who is not used to being fit can lose weight quicker because there body is not used to the exercise. That's why you see people on TV talk shows that lost 150 pounds in a year. If I wanted to really lose weight, I would have to take some drastic measures.

Okay, who am I kidding? Yeah, it might be true that there are some factors that make it more difficult for me to loose the weight, but was that really what was stopping me? I was at it again, making excuses for being fat. Either I was going to do something about it or not. Bottom line. No in between. No excuses.

Pushing 200

I was walking on campus one day when I saw Boris and a few of his boys. I didn't really want to be seen with him on campus, but I couldn't help but remember how kind and loving he had been toward me at a time when I really needed it. It had been a while since I had seen him, so I reached out to give him a hug and he engulfed me in a passionate embrace. After the basic chitchat we went our separate ways. One of the boys he was with dropped a pen. When I turned to pick it up and take it to him their backs were turned to me. The boy who dropped the pen said to Boris, "Man, you love those girls that are pushing two hundred don't you?" I was enraged. What did he mean by "pushing two hundred?" I only weighed…. 185. He was right. But he didn't have to say it. Just for that, I was going to keep his pen.

Sexy as a Swine

As my weight increased and my confidence declined my sex drive began to take the plunge as well. I didn't feel sexy anymore. I even got to the point where I was ashamed to undress with the lights on so I would always make sure that the room was dark before engaged in love making. There are certain things that you can hide with clothes on that cannot be concealed when you are naked. Control top panty hose and girdles are far from being considered sexy lingerie.

Davin went to a black engineering conference in Chicago. He called me when he got there and I jokingly told him that he better bring me back a souvenir. When he told me that he had already got something for me, I was looking forward to the shot glass, key chain, hat or t-shirt that I though he might be bringing back for me. When he got home, he came over that night to bring me my souvenir. I reached in the shiny gift bag that was extremely light. When I pushed the tissue paper aside I felt something small, smooth and slinky. He bought a lingerie set for me from the Victoria's Secret store on the

The Ups and Downs of Being Round
Monica Marie Jones

Magnificent Mile. It was a lavender demi styled bra trimmed in lace with a thong to match.

Instinct told me that it would probably not fit but I tried it on anyway so that Davin's feeling would not be hurt. The only person's whose feelings ended up getting hurt were my own. When I tried on the thong, it fit but the sides were cutting into my hips and my belly was covering the lace trim on the top. When I tried on the bra, it was too tight. Not only did I have boob spillage, but my right areola kept playing peek-a-boo.

He meant well. I'm sure he was looking forward to seeing his woman in some sexy lingerie, but the feelings that I was experiencing at that moment were far from sexy. For me, sexiness was a feeling of the past.

I used to be limber and petite. I could ride a man into the sunset without breaking a sweat. Now my movements were labored and I lost the flexibility that I had acquired during my dancing days. I held back on the grinding that I really desired to do because I didn't want to suffocate my lover. Poor Davin. He was the best man that I had ever had and he was not getting the best of me. Lovers of the past would go on and on about how good I was in the sack, but Davin couldn't even experience it because of my sexual insecurities.

With all of my boobs, my inflamed inner thighs and everything else, Davin loved me for who I was no matter what. This was great in that it taught me that love and beauty went beyond the surface of the skin and flesh. The bad news was that it made me comfortable…too comfortable.

The Body of a woman

The Ups and Downs of Being Round
Monica Marie Jones

"You are a woman now, so you have the body of a woman. You were a child then. You cannot expect to have a child's body anymore." That was the first "I'm trying to make you feel better about your weight," statement from Jaynelle that actually made me feel a little better. For a while I stopped worrying about my weight. After all I had found a man who liked me for me no matter what. With that I tried to make the best out of my situation. These days there were plenty of plus sized women who were successful, beautiful, and appeared to be quite confident. Unfortunately, if they were anything like me that confidence was just an act to mask the struggles on the inside.

I worried too much of what others thought of me. Ever since I was a child I had the misconstrued notion that everyone was looking at me, thinking about me, and judging me because of how I looked. I finally realized that people have their own problems and better things to do than worry about me. Although to this day I still have a small portion of that mindset buried in the back of my brain. I guess you could call it my inner fat child. I realized how much I looked up to and respected strong and beautiful sisters like Queen Latifah and Missy Elliot. They were fabulous in my eyes no matter what. Their size didn't make me admire them any less. I decided that I would try to make the best of my size and accept the fact that I was destined to be a big woman.

I had been hearing the term full figured thrown around. At first it was in reference to Tyra Banks because she was a size 8, which was considered big for a model. I thought, "Oh great, if a size 8 is full figured then I must be overflow figured." Then I came across an ad

The Ups and Downs of Being Round
Monica Marie Jones

for full figured models in Ebony Magazine and the women in the pictures actually looked like everyday large women. As I read the small print I realized that I was not big enough to fit their stipulations! According to their guidelines their models had to be at least 5'8 and wear a size 18 or higher. I was in large lady limbo. It should have made me feel good that I was actually too small for something, but more than anything it made me confused. I didn't want to aspire to be bigger to fit the full figured model mold, but I was far from the mini model mold as well.

In the meantime I just decided to find comfort right where I was at. I didn't feel like stressing out about what I ate or how much I exercised. I just wanted to be. It didn't do drugs or drink alcohol. What was so wrong with enjoying a good meal every now and then? So for months I went on without a care in the world. My comfort with my size turned out to be merely a passing phase once I entered the work world.

Part Four:

Young Adulthood

"A Lifestyle Change"

CHAPTER NINE

Childhood revisited

After college I got a job as a teacher. I taught during the day and took classes toward my Masters degree at night. I was so tired at the end of my day that I had just enough time to bathe, study, prepare for the next day, and eat. I always made sure to make time to eat. Due to my lack of time, I ended up cutting exercise from my schedule. I would much rather use any extra time I had catching up on much needed sleep. Graduate school was kicking my behind. It was the most stressful experience of my life. I turned to food for comfort and it soothed me. I found myself reasoning, "I need some Reese's Pieces to calm my nerves," or, "a Snickers bar is brain food." I loved teaching and that brought balance to my hatred for graduate school.

My rising stress level and reliance on food for comfort added another 20 pounds to my small frame. It also pushed me over the dreaded 200-pound mark. On top of all of that, I acquired a sweet/salt/sour complex. This means that I could not just snack on potato chips and be satisfied. After the salty taste of the chips, I felt the need to counter the taste with something sweet like chocolate. I then had to counter the sweetness with something sour or fruity sweet like Sour Patch Kids or Skittles. It was a ritual that I had to go through whenever I snacked. Every time I bought snacks I had to buy them in threes. It was pathetic. I'm not sure how I acquired that silly habit, but I did not feel satisfied without practicing it.

The Ups and Downs of Being Round
Monica Marie Jones

My job as a teacher was wonderful and rewarding, but I slowly began to realize that the cruelty I had experienced in my own childhood had come full circle. Children mean well, but can be brutally honest. We teach them that it is wrong to lie, so how is it that we can get mad at them for telling the truth?

It was a Tuesday morning. We were learning about Mr. S with his slouching socks of the Alphabet People. My kindergarteners are such a joy to be around. I feel so relaxed with them. I walked around the classroom surveying everyone's handwriting as they attempted to create the letter *S* like a slithering snake as I had instructed. When I got to Angie's desk she looked up then put her hand on my stomach and with the most sincerely surprised face said, "Miss Jenson, are you pregnant?" I guess I was too relaxed because when I looked down at my stomach I realized why Angie had said what she said. There it was, round and poked out like I was in the second trimester of a pregnancy. In all of my comfort, I had forgotten to hold my stomach in like I normally did.

That incident drove me back to my endless cycle of dieting and trying to lose weight. I bought cases of Slim Fast and would drink them at work, trying to disguise them by wrapping paper towel around the can or pouring its contents into a coffee mug. The only problem was that I drank them as the beverage with my meals instead of using them to replace the meal. On my way home from work that night I went to the library and checked out a few diet books in an attempt to do some research.

The book that I was reading told me to keep a picture posted of what I used to look like to motivate me to get to where I wanted to be.

The Ups and Downs of Being Round
Monica Marie Jones

I had my high school prom picture on my desk at work to serve as my motivation. I wore a slinky, long, fitted red dress with sheer material over my back and stomach. The dress clung to me and showed off my thin, curvaceous figure.

Some people had been big all of their lives, but I had the past knowledge that I could drop pounds, which kept my spirits high. My pleasant thoughts were interrupted as one of my students (Randy) approached my desk to get a Kleenex. He caught a glimpse of a picture of me and said, "Miss Jenson, you used to be skinny."

As if that wasn't enough to crush my ego, he yelled to Regan to come see the picture of Miss Jenson when she used to be pretty. I felt like crying. That was the way I had always dealt with it when I was younger. The truth was that no matter what my body looked like on the outside, I always had the self-esteem of the little fat girl on the inside.

Crying was no longer an acceptable form of showing my emotions. This was not a good idea in front of a room full of kindergarteners. They would have burst out crying at the site of my tears. I didn't cry, but viewed it as yet another wake up call. I firmly told Randy and Regan to take their seats and grabbed my dictionary to look up the word "hunger."

Most of the definitions referred to food, but one in particular caught my eye. It said *to desire with great eagerness*. This made me think - hunger is not always about food. Maybe I am hungry for something else. I was determined to find out. I was, 24 years old and I didn't know myself.

Health Concerns

The Ups and Downs of Being Round
Monica Marie Jones

I had control of everything else in my life now it was time to take control of my body, and more importantly, my health. At 5'2 inches tall and over two hundred pounds, I was at high risk for all of the fatal diseases related to obesity and they all ran in my immediate family - diabetes, high blood pressure, and hypertension. My mother, grandmother, uncle and grandfather all suffered from these health issues. The health risks were motivation enough, but there were other deep-seated issues burning at my core.

Granny drawers

That Christmas, Davin and I went to my grandmother's house to celebrate. Among the several knickknacks and other items I received, grandma bought me some humongous bloomers. The kind of big granny drawers you point and laugh at in the stores. When Davin and I got back to my apartment that night he helped me to put away the gifts that I had received from my family. When we came across the granny drawers we laughed hysterically as I held them against my pelvis. I tried them on to see how foolish I looked as they fell back down around my ankles. At once all of the laughing ceased and we were stricken with uncomfortable silence. The panties did not fall to my ankles, they fit, snuggly. I was humiliated.

Being overweight a second time was far more stressful than being overweight all of your life. The anguish is greater because once you've had a taste of the "thin" life it is difficult to go back to the way things used to be. It's like being poor, working hard, starting that reaps millions of dollars, then losing the fortune. The changes may not be obvious right away, but before you know it you are back to

The Ups and Downs of Being Round
Monica Marie Jones

being broke. It's worse than having been poor your whole life because you have had a taste of the good life.

Many poor people are happy as they are because they know no other way of living. Once you cross over into a new standard of living, going in reverse is pure hell. This is how it feels to be fat, then skinny, then fat all over again. It eats away at you because you know what you could be; perhaps even having the pictures as a constant nagging reminder of your former self.

I created several excuses to make myself feel better. I had to find things that would help me to keep up the front that I was confident. The truth was that the only person that I had to convince that I was confident was myself. But I would look at other women who weighed far more than me and rationalize, "at least I am not as big as she is." Or I would reduce the foods I ate to make my self believe that they were not as bad for me as they really were. "French fries are made from potatoes, so they are really a vegetable." " Raisinettes have raisins in them the so they are really a fruit." "Reese's Pieces have peanut butter in them which comes from peanuts, so they are a good source of protein." I could find ingredients in any food and convince myself that it was in some way, healthy.

Let love be the reason

My resolve to make a change was strengthened by my relationship with Davin. He was so good to me. I found it hard to accept his love for me. I felt as if the relationship was too good to be true. For the first year of our relationship, I was terrified that something horrible was going to happen to me because there was no way that I deserved such goodness in my life. I had gotten used to

The Ups and Downs of Being Round
Monica Marie Jones

feeling under appreciated and being verbally abused by the men I had dated in the past. Davin graduated with his MBA a year before I graduated with my Master's degree and landed a plush and cushy job straight out of school. When I graduated a year later, he decided to take me on my dream vacation as a graduation gift.

My dream had always been to go to Disney World. Davin made that dream come true for me. I graduated in December so we went for the Christmas holiday. On Christmas day we decided to go to the Magic Kingdom. That night we watched the fireworks show over Cinderella's Castle. I was mesmerized at the way the colorful bursts danced against the clear night sky in sync with the Christmas carols playing on the loud speakers. I was awakened from my trance like state because I could have sworn I heard Mickey Mouse called my name.

"I must be too caught up in the magic of the moment," I thought to myself. I was probably just going into sensory overload like I used to back in my younger days at the Michigan State Fair. Just as I settled back in to my daze, I heard it again, this time loud and clear. "Will Madison Jenson and Davin Strickland please join us on the stage." I looked at Davin in bewilderment. Had he heard or was I just going crazy because I was so caught up in the moment? He did not return my gaze because he had grabbed my hand and was trying to lead me through the crowd up to the stage. Once we got on the stage, Mickey announced that Davin had a magical wish that only Madison could make come true. At this point Davin was already on one knee when he took the microphone from Mickey and said, "Madison, will

The Ups and Downs of Being Round
Monica Marie Jones

you make my dream come true and do me the great honor of being my wife?"

A hush came over the crowd as they waited with baited breath for my response. At the same moment, a warm salty tear reached my lip. I found the strength to vocalize what my heart had been screaming. "Yes, Davin, I would love to be your wife, yes!" The crowd erupted in a mixture of "oohs," "awwwws," and thunderous applause. At that moment, *When You Wish Upon a Star* began to melodically float from the loud speakers and manufactured snow began to fall.

The final wake up call

When we got back home from Disney World I was still reeling. I was so excited that I could not wait another moment to see the pictures that we had taken. On the way home we went to the store and put the film in for 1 hour development and shopped for popcorn and other snacks to munch on while we watched the home video that we had filmed while on vacation. Once we got our pictures and snacks, we headed home and snuggled up on the couch to watch our video.

I completely lost my appetite when I say myself in the video. I did not realize how huge I appeared to the world until I saw that tape. I paused the tape, grabbed the pictures that we had just gotten developed and ran into the bathroom and locked the door. A confused Davin came running after me and began banging on the door to see what was wrong with me. I tuned him out as I hurriedly shuffled through the photographs.

Certainly my eyes must have deceived me when I saw myself on the videotape, so I needed to see my self in the pictures to confirm

The Ups and Downs of Being Round
Monica Marie Jones

what I already knew to be true. As I flipped through picture after picture it became more and more clear to me. This had gone too far. It was time to make a change in my life.

CHAPTER TEN

Soul Journey

Davin and I decided to move in together to save money for the wedding, although some members of our families looked down on "shacking up." Davin treated me like I was a beautiful Queen. It felt like the days when I was little and people used to give me compliments that I didn't believe. What did he see in me that was so beautiful? He deserved better. He deserved a girl that felt and looked beautiful inside and out. I loved him too much to let him go to find that girl, so I decided that I would make myself become that girl.

More importantly it was time for me to start loving myself. I couldn't love anyone else before I knew, accepted, and loved myself first. And besides all of that, I wanted to look good in my wedding dress. The wedding was scheduled for October 1st two years following the proposal This gave us more than enough time to properly plan and save the money we needed to make it an extravagant event. It also gave me time to get myself together. I decided to wear my mother's wedding dress as an inspiration to get myself in shape. She was a size 6 when she got married. Currently I was a size 16. I knew that I had a lot of work ahead of me, but I had two years, and lots of drive. This time it would be different. I had a few other things to work on besides my physique if I wanted to be successful. I would not be simply focused on the weight, but I would get on a path to self-discovery and healing in mind, body and spirit. I would call it my "soul journey."

Successfully achieving my goals would call for a major lifestyle change. The first thing that I had to do was to accept myself in

The Ups and Downs of Being Round
Monica Marie Jones

my current state of fatness. It had always been a part of me, so I accepted it and made it a part of my identity. Except I would not be fat, I would be "phat." Feminists had changed the term *history* to *herstory,* homosexual's embraced that which was once meant to insult them in the term *Queer,* and African Americans had taken the word *nigger*, renamed it *nigga*, and began using it as a term of endearment. I too would take control from the oppressor and give positive power to the negative connotations of the vocabulary that was once meant to destroy me.

I accepted phatness as a part of my identity, but it didn't mean that I had to live life overweight and eat whatever I wanted. Health and having control of one's life was important to me. I first had to come to terms with why I ate. I realized that I was eating for far more than simply nourishing my body. I also ate when I was bored, stressed, happy, nervous, to reward myself, and during breakfast, lunch, and dinner. I ate all of the time. Ever since I read that definition for hunger, I realized that I was hungry for more than just food. I was hungry for self-acceptance and used food as a crutch.

I was a food head - similar to a crack head with the only difference being that food was my drug of choice. I think crack heads have it easier because a human can live and function perfectly without crack, but without food, a person can die. There is not as much support out there for a person that is addicted to food. We don't have foodaholics anonymous meetings readily at our disposal.

"Hi my name is Madison, and I am a foodaholic," would never fall from my lips in a room of likeminded ones. I am sure the meetings exist somewhere, but are not easily accessible. Anorexia and

The Ups and Downs of Being Round
Monica Marie Jones

bulimia are taken seriously as eating disorders for which treatment and therapy is readily available. Overeating, a disorder just the same, is looked upon as shameful, gluttonous and a mere lack of will power and self control. We, the overeaters, are left to find comfort and support in food.

I decided to take matters into my own hands. The first thing I did was to get the devil out of my house. "Potato chips, twinkies, French fries, butter pecan ice cream, and chocolate, I rebuke you in the name of thinness!"

I liked to ride the white horse, but wasn't addicted to cocaine. I was addicted to white foods. This meant anything that contained white flour or white sugar. I could live on pasta and bread alone. I thought that these foods were healthy since they weren't high in fat or calories. I never would have thought that these were probably what was adding pounds to my thighs.

These foods may not have been harmful in moderation, but I constantly ate them in large and heaping portions. The next thing I did was to get rid of the abundance of processed carbohydrates. I replaced them with whole grains and carbohydrates in their natural forms. I replaced the white with brown - brown sugar and rice, unbleached wheat flour, and whole wheat bread. A lot of my eating habits were due to ignorance. I lacked the knowledge about foods and what they can do to you. I educated myself about food, nutrition, and dieting.

I read every diet book, health magazine, nutrition book, watched tons of videos, and started reading all of the labels and ingredients before I bought or ate food.

The Ups and Downs of Being Round
Monica Marie Jones

    The changes that I was beginning to make in my life were not easy. After two weeks of eating healthy, I went through carbohydrate withdrawal. I was at home watching television. I wasn't even hungry, just bored. I grabbed a snack - a gourmet cracker. One cracker wouldn't hurt anything, I thought. It was light, delicious and buttery with just the right amount of salt. That one cracker was a trigger setting my carbohydrate cravings in overdrive. I kept on eating one cracker after another until before I knew it I had eaten the whole box was empty. I still craved a peanut butter and jelly sandwich afterwards.

    What was wrong with me? I couldn't control myself. I wanted any and every snack I could get my hands on. I started getting nervous and began to cry. I didn't want it to be like every other time where I told people, "I'm on a diet and this time I'm for real." I didn't want to speak about it, I wanted to be about it, and here I was about to throw it all way. I prayed and decided that I would fix myself a healthy meal and if I still wasn't satisfied after that, drink with water until there was no room for anything else to fit. I fixed a large plate of salad with cucumbers, tomatoes, and green peppers, then prepared brown rice with grilled chicken wings and steamed broccoli and carrots. After I was done eating I had a craving for sweets, so I drank a cup of tea sweetened with honey. I got the largest cup I could find in the house and filled it with water. I drank and drank until I was about to burst. My craving finally subsided.

    I knew that I would need support from people because I didn't want to go thru any more withdrawal episodes alone. Another incident like that would surely trigger a nervous breakdown. I read the personal weight loss testimonies and success stories of people who lost weight and kept it off. I surrounded myself with positive people who would truly encourage me. Then I plastered the cabinet and refrigerator doors with pictures of me in my slim days, motivational quotes, and a list of my fitness goals.

Madison's work out plan

The next thing that I did was join a women's only local fitness center called Shapely Lady. I didn't need to feel uncomfortable or self-conscious about men watching me. I didn't want them to see me trip because I missed a step on the treadmill or watch my boobs and booty bounce as I ran around the track. I signed a contract for a one year paid membership to motivate me to keep going. When it comes to money, I don't play. I work too hard for it to see it go down the drain. I was going to get every penny's worth. The center had drawings and prizes as incentives for losing weight. It may sound silly but I am a very competitive person and I love to win. Even if it is a t-shirt or a bumper sticker, I will work hard to lose extra pounds to be the winner. The center weighed and measured you each month to chart your progress. This was another great motivational tool because I needed to feel like I was accomplishing something. The household scale is not a reliable motivator. It was nice to know that I was losing inches and body fat, things that the scale at home could not measure.

On the first day I went in for my initial measurement and weigh in. I thought that I was around 210. I watched as the girl who was helping me slowly scooted it past 210 up to 214. I couldn't believe it! This was the highest weight that I had ever been! When

The Ups and Downs of Being Round
Monica Marie Jones

she did my measurements, they looked more like a man's dimensions than a woman's.

The first day that I stepped into the fitness center after my initial weigh-in, I felt like a kid again entering the first day of dance class. I had on some baggy cotton pants and a huge t-shirt to cover up my extra rolls. This was much better than that dreadful day in dance class many years ago because this time I was not the only one overweight. As I looked around the room I saw women of all different shapes, sizes, ages and colors. It was inspiring to see a woman that looked to be in her 70's working out with the rest of us, and another who was over 300 pounds, sweating it out. It felt good surrounded by all of these women who had similar goals as me. I observed each woman and created their personal stories in my head.

The woman who weighed over three hundred pounds would probably do anything just to get down to my size. She wanted to look more like the girl who had on the short running shorts and sports bra. And the elderly lady most likely wanted the youthfulness that we all had.

One lady in particular caught my eye. She was in her late thirties to early forties and was super skinny. I was wondering why she was working out. I kept staring at her. Maybe she had one of those disorders where she thinks she is fat so she exercises excessively, I thought. My inquisitiveness began got the best of me, so I went over and asked her why.

"Hi, my name is Madison, and I hope you don't mind me asking, but why are you here?"

The Ups and Downs of Being Round
Monica Marie Jones

"Oh no, I don't mind at all. Hi. My name is Geneva, and thank you for being so generous and kind to call me thin. Most people prefer the terms, skinny, beanpole, bag of bones…and the list goes on. I'm here for the strength training component because I want to gain weight and build muscle."

Gain weight? Had I heard her correctly? It felt like a slap in the face that we all were trying to lose weight, and she was trying to gain. I felt myself getting upset but decided to hear her out. I doubted that there could be any logical reasoning behind it. Who in their right mind would want to *gain* weight?

She continued, "You see, I have been skinny all my life. And I have always been picked on, teased and ignored because of it. I've tried everything to gain weight from taking weight gain pills, to protein shakes…you name it, I've tried it. But nothing worked."

"I would sit in bars and be completely invisible to the opposite sex. The only time I was acknowledged was when someone would make a comment like, 'she is too skinny.' 'Cause for black women, thin is not in, black men like their women with some curves. I did meet and marry someone, but the final straw came when that very same marriage ended as a result of my weight, or lack thereof. That's when I knew for sure that I had to do something about it. That's why I joined. This place helps those who are underweight to build up muscle and gain mass. I want curves too."

I was speechless. I never would have thought that underweight people shared the insecurities and low self esteem that overweight people did. It reminded me of the conversation that I had with Katrina

The Ups and Downs of Being Round
Monica Marie Jones

back in the day about how people with short hair and darker skin have the same insecurities and feelings as their polar opposites.

It's an endless cycle. Everyone wants to be something that they are not. No one seems to be happy where they are although there might be someone else that would be perfectly happy to walk through life in their shoes. Where does this cyclical torture stem from? Why is it so hard for us to accept and love ourselves as we are?

Hello, my name is Madison, and I'm an overeater

The day after I joined the gym, I was browsing through the paper and came across an advertisement for a support group. The group was called Food Addicts in Recovery. The world was finally starting to realize that the addiction to food is a real problem. The ad read:

Anonymous (FA) is a 12-step program to help people suffering from overeating, bulimia, and anorexia. No dues, fees or weigh-ins.

Every Monday night at 6pm,

Church of Love in God.

I didn't really appreciate the fact that all three disorders were lumped together. I felt that each problem should be addressed separately. Bulimia and anorexia had their own special treatments and clinics. Could the overeaters just get a little love and attention by having a treatment program specifically designed for them? I appreciate the acknowledgement of overeating as a disorder but I wished there were things out there that were specifically intended for us.

Maybe If the group was just for overeaters, I would have joined but it wasn't. I decided to pass. I couldn't sit in a room full of skinny people and pretend to understand what they were going through. And there was no way they could understand what I was going through. I would probably be the only overeater present. I knew that there were weight loss support groups, but I wanted to dig deep and get behind WHY I gained the weight in the first place.

CHAPTER ELEVEN

The weigh-in

I had my weigh-in and measure day. I was nervous because I have kept organized track of that. I would just jump on and off of the scale whenever I felt the urge. Sometimes I would weigh myself three times a day. It fascinated me how my weight could fluctuate to an eight-pound difference from morning to night. It varied based on how I ate, how much water I drank, or whether I used the bathroom or not. At other times, I could go for days or weeks without weighing myself, because I knew the number was not decreasing but climbing constantly, and it would depress me.

I was shocked to find out that my beginning weight was 214. I was interested to see what the results would be today. When I woke up, I didn't eat or drink. In fact, I didn't eat or drink anything after 7 p.m. the night before. When I used the bathroom, I squeezed every morsel out of my body that I could. I wore the most form fitting exercise gear that I could find. I didn't want to add any extra inches by wearing the baggy clothes that I usually wore to hide my bulge.

When I arrived, I was tempted to weigh myself first for if I had failed to lose weight, I reasoned that I would not go through with weigh-in. But I just decided to have some faith in myself and do the weigh-in.

I approached my personal fitness coach and let her know that it was my scheduled day to get weighed and measured. She pulled my file and gathered all of the tools that she needed. The tools were a

The Ups and Downs of Being Round
Monica Marie Jones

yellow tape measure and a white apparatus that looked like a big video game joystick. The first area that she measured was my bust.

"Wow! Do you have on a different bra from the last time you weighed in?" She asked in astonishment.

"No, why do you ask?"

"Because you have lost 3 inches in your bust, that is amazing!"

"Oh." Was all that I could manage to say. I was flattered by the compliment but my feelings were mixed. My breasts had always been my claim to fame, especially since I was lacking in the booty department. But they were so big lately that they had become uncomfortable. But my bras were fitting a lot looser than normal. Usually it felt like the under-wire was cutting to the meat. Now they were leaning closer to the side of feeling just right.

I fought the urge to suck in my stomach as she measured the rest of my body. She moved from my chest to my abdomen, waist, hips, arms and thighs. I had lost inches in each area. Then it was time to get weighed on the scale. As we approached the scale, I felt like I was walking the green mile. It all seemed to take place in slow motion. All of the sucking, tucking and hiding in the world would not change the reading of my weight. "There is no possibility that I can strip down naked?" I asked jokingly. But in the back of my mind I was half serious because if we weren't in public, I would have done anything to weigh a few ounces less than before.

I took a deep breath before I stepped on. She slid the bottom marker to the 150-pound mark. And the scale measuring stick dropped to the bottom with a thud. I was not disappointed yet because it would have been unrealistic to drop that much weight in a month. Next she moved the bottom marker to the 200 mark and slid the top one to the 14. This time the stick popped to the top. She moved the top marker back until it reached 207 pounds. After the first month I had lost a total seven pounds and eight inches. I was happy because I didn't expect to do that well.

I couldn't hide my excitement on my way back to the table where the measurement tools were placed. Next, she entered some information into a big, white joystick and had me hold it out at arms length. This calculated my body fat percentage. I had lost 1.5% body fat. It didn't sound like a lot to me but according to her, it was good progress for only having been at it for one month. After my workout, my coach had a printout ready for me that showed a graph and chart of my progress. Before handing it to me she announced my progress to everyone. All of the women were clapping and congratulating me. I fought the feeling to take a bow. I wasn't used to all this praise and encouragement. I was used to people who were glad to see me fail. I sucked all of the positive energy in and walked out of the building with my head held high and my shrunken chest poked out.

Releasing the weight

With each passing month, my weigh-in days followed the same pattern. I would lose six to eight pounds and a few inches. I noticed that my clothes were fitting looser and I had a lot more energy. I also felt various parts of my body becoming more firm and toned. The changes that were happening to my body were actually kind of funny. I was losing a lot of weight and inches in my upper and lower body but my middle was staying the same. My stomach to boob ratio was embarrassingly disproportionate. If I didn't suck my stomach in with all of my might, my stomach would stick out farther than my breasts.

Bad Hair Days

I made another change in my life along with my new commitment to a healthy lifestyle. I decided to go natural with my hair. I had worn a perm for years and as a result, my hair would never grow past a certain point. My combs, brushes, and clothing were full of strands of my hair that had broken off because of the harsh chemicals in the perms. My hair always had a dull and dead look. It would drink up any grease that I put on it and dry again. It was an endless cycle. If I got a perm too soon, my hair would begin to break off. If I waited too long to get a perm, my hair would break. It was a no- win situation. I decided to get off of the chemical merry go round. It turned out that it was not as easy as I thought it would be.

After a few months of going natural, I couldn't take it anymore. My roots were so nappy and unmanageable that I resorted to wearing hats and scarves all of the time. So I decided to get a mild perm. Once I put it in, I regretted my choice instantly. My hair didn't look all that hot. Three weeks later it started falling out in clumps. This was the final straw. I cut it all off at the new growth and got micro braid extensions the next day.

No one knew that I looked like a honeydew melon with a buzz cut underneath all of those braids. I wanted to have natural hair, but for me that meant no chemicals. I didn't have the head size or the face to sport one of those short, natural hair styles. My head was too big and

The Ups and Downs of Being Round
Monica Marie Jones

my face too round. That type of style only looked cute on women with small heads and sleek faces like Jada Pinkett Smith.

Those braids saved my life; they also were a blessing because with all of my working out, my hair would have constantly been a mess from all of the sweat. The braids kept me looking brand new. I continued to get braids for the next year and a half. By the time I was ready to unleash my new all natural mane it was thick, healthy, well past my shoulders and creeping down my back. I thought I had a lot of hair before, but I had even more now. The next day I went on a hunt for an older black beautician who specialized in the press and curl. No one knows how to tame the wildest mane with a little bergamot and a hard press like an older black woman.

My new hairdo added more confidence to my already growing self-esteem. At first I was worried about it sweating out during my workouts, but I soon learned that if my hair was trained and pressed hard enough, it could withstand anything. I wrapped my hair around my head, tied it with a satin scarf, and worked out per usual. When I was done, I gave it time to dry while it still wrapped. Once combed, it would be as beautiful and shiny as the day that it was done. If that method didn't work, I would touch up the edges with a pressing comb and flat iron the rest. At this point, how my body looked was far more important to me tha how my hair looked.

Overall, my natural coif gave me more freedom for versatility. I could have straight hair on Monday, Afro puffs on Tuesday, cornrows on Wednesday, and tight curly tendrils on Thursday. The thickness made it hard to deal with but the new health, length, and versatility was worth it.

CHAPTER 12

The flip side of fat

Life is completely different on the flip side of fat. I was now down to a size 8, which was small compared to the size 16 I used to be. Technically that meant that I was half of my former self. All of the attention that I had been getting from men let me know that I was looking fine in their eyes. I was not used to this. It felt good and I was definitely flattered. I had the urge to go out lately and show off the new me. I thought that I had gotten over the clubbing stage of my life – but I was wrong. I had that itch again.

Scratching the itch

The opportunity to scratch my itch came sooner than I thought it would. After getting my Masters degree and putting in a full two school years at my job, I accepted a more lucrative teaching position in Detroit. It was a 100-mile roundtrip commute, but the increase in salary made it worthwhile.

A few months into my time working there, the gym teacher, Raymond asked if I would like to join him and the basketball coach, Tone, for drinks after work on Thursday, I thought, "why not?" I along with two 2nd grade teachers, Rashida and Lena, were invited.

As a kindergarten teacher, I never really got to wear the clothes that I wanted to, so I used this as an opportunity to show off my new, more stylish, size 8 clothing. I wore a stretch denim one-piece pantsuit, tight and buttoned up in the front. I left a few of the top buttons open to show a little cleavage. I was proud that my cleavage looked more classy than sleazy.

The Ups and Downs of Being Round
Monica Marie Jones

This denim outfit was a major triumph for me because a little over a year ago, I tried one on in a size large and got stuck. I had to summon Davin into the ladies dressing room to pry me out of it. Talk about embarrassing! Now I was fitting comfortably into a smaller size of the exact same outfit.

That night we all drove separate cars and met in front of the school. When we got there we all turned our windows down and discussed the travel arrangements. We decided that it would be more fun if we all rode together. We parked our individual cars and piled into Raymond's Excursion. When I stepped out of the car, I felt Raymond and Tone checking me out. They had never seen me dressed like this because my usual daily attire consisted of long, loose jumper dresses with apples and little red schoolhouses embroidered on the front pocket. I zeroed in on Tone's lips just in time to catch him mouthing the word "WOW!"

The reaction that I got from my co-workers overwhelmed me. I felt uncomfortable but extremely flattered. These feelings were all new to me. It had been a long time since I had felt anything like it. The situation reminded me of a scene from the movie Waiting to Exhale where the character Gloria felt her suitor watching her from behind so she put a little extra swagger in her step. Before I knew it, I found myself doing the same thing.

When we got into the truck I sat in the back with Rashida and Lena and the guys sat in the front. I had not been in a social situation with anyone other than Davin since college, so I felt nervous and wasn't quite sure how to act. I sat quietly with my hands clasped together tightly. Rashida and Lena had hung out together previously

The Ups and Downs of Being Round
Monica Marie Jones

with them, so they were chatting away as Tone was bobbed his head to the song that was on the radio. Raymond broke the ice by asking the question, "So, are you ladies involved?" Rashida answered immediately, "There is no ring on my finger!" Lena followed by responding, "I have a friend, but we have an understanding." I decided not to volunteer any information if I was not forced to when Tone chimed in and asked, "What about you Madison?" Normally I would have quickly and proudly announced that I was engaged while simultaneously showing off my ring. This time it was different. I felt ashamed that I was in a serious relationship. I wanted to lie and say that I just had a boyfriend, or that I was single. But I decided against it because I was already feeling bad that I had somewhat misled Davin for the first time in our relationship.

I told him that I was going out with some co-workers, knowing full well that he assumed that all of these "co-worker" were females. I knew this because as I was leaving our apartment that morning he said, "have fun with your girls." I didn't bother to correct him or volunteer the information that males would be in attendance. I quickly answered by saying "I'm engaged," before something that I regretted slipped out of my mouth. I saw a hint of disappointment in Tone's eyes.

The guys paid our way into the club and made sure that we were straight on drinks all night. We all hung together but other men in the club realized that I was not officially tied to either of the men in our group and tried to pull me away all night. Whenever this happened, Tone would slip his arm around my waist and start dancing with me to rescue me. I realized that for once I was not self-conscious

The Ups and Downs of Being Round
Monica Marie Jones

about someone grabbing me around the waist fearing that they may grab a hold of one of the rolls that I was forever attempting to conceal.

This had been my first time in a club since my new weight loss and it was almost overwhelming. Men were offering to buy me drinks and I was so excited that I accepted every single one. I noticed that women were cutting their eyes at me. I downed drink after drink with haste to help me cope with everything that was taking place.

Before I knew it I was grinding with Tone to the pulsating beats of the bass emanating from the speakers, which magnified the buzz that had my head spinning. The next thing that I remember is being pressed up against Tone on the side of Raymond's truck telling him how much I was feeling him. I looked to my right and Raymond was pressed up against Lena on the other side of the truck and Rashida was passed out and sprawled across the back seat. The last thing that I remembered clearly was slowly drifting in and out of consciousness myself.

Fade in: I was riding in Raymond's car wrapped in Tone's arms. *Fade out.*

Fade In: I was strewn over Tone's shoulder and he had my car keys and purse in his other hand. I felt happy that I was light enough to be carried by a man. *Fade out.*

Fade in: I was in Tone's bedroom.

That woke me up really quickly. "Where am I," I managed to mouth with the little bit of saliva that was left.

"You are at my apartment. You were too drunk to drive all the way back to Ypsilanti. You gave me your car keys, don't you remember?" Tone asked.

The Ups and Downs of Being Round
Monica Marie Jones

Thoughts and memories of the night before began to flood my brain all at once and became a jumbled cluster. I tried to connect the gaps, fill in the holes and fit the missing pieces of the puzzle to no avail. The last thing that I could clearly remember was grinding and sweating on the dance floor with Tone and now I was in his bed. Suddenly reality hit me like a brick.

"Oh my God, Davin!!!" I tried to remember if I had called him or not to let him know my whereabouts, but how in the world could I tell him that I was in the bed of another man? That was when it occurred to me that I had told Davin that I would be spending the night at Jaynelle's house. I really had planned to so that I wouldn't have to make the long ride home tired and tipsy, but who knew that it would turn out to be my alibi?

"Tone... did we... do....anything?"

Tone looked at me with a straight face and said, "Well, it depends on what you mean by anything."

I nervously responded, "You know, like...sex?"

"Well, I don't know if we could exactly call it sex, I mean we started out with a couple of harmless dips, which led to a few full strokes...but then you kinda freaked out. You said you shouldn't be doing this and rolled out of the bed and started crying."

What had I done? Everything started to race through my mind. Davin and I were engaged, we had a bank account together, furniture, and I had thrown that all away by cheating, and for what? Just because men were starting to pay me some attention because I lost weight. Then another disturbing thought occurred to me. Tone probably never would have given me the time of day before I lost all of the weight. I was confused and overwhelmed by my emotions that I burst out crying again and jumped out of the bed. I got dressed quickly and ran out of Tone's place without looking back.

A change occurs

When I got home after work the next day, I knew that things would never be the same. I could barely look Davin in the eye. I used to spend all of my free time doing research, planning and preparing for the wedding, but now, I had lost all interest in that. When Davin asked me about my night out with my co-workers I put on a fake smile and told him the edited version of the fun we had. I told him about all of the attention that I was getting from guys thinking that he would be flattered that other men found his woman to be attractive. When I saw his facial expression I knew that I was wrong. I had never seen that look on his face before. It was a strange look, one that I couldn't quite place. It let me know to be careful what I shared in the future.

Just when my emotions and self-esteem were beginning to rise because of my weight loss, they took a mean blow from my indiscretions. Instead of vowing never to do it again, I continued to go out with my co-workers and see Tone. I would just get as drunk as possible so I wouldn't have to deal with it.

Ever since I shared that bit of information with Davin about men giving me attention, he seemed to become more and more distant and less supportive of me and my weight loss efforts. This pushed me deeper into my deceitful actions and destructive behavior. I was leading a dual life. In Ypsilanti, I was the nice innocent wife-playing house. But when I was in Detroit, I was a fast girl living a life without boundaries.

The Ups and Downs of Being Round
Monica Marie Jones

That year Davin and I decided to take a trip to New York to celebrate my birthday with a little shopping and clubbing. It started out great, but that all changed on the night of my birthday when we went to a popular nightclub to celebrate. I was drinking and dancing the night away and I guess a little bit of the Detroit side of my life started to show. Other guys were on me all night, regardless of the fact that I was there with Davin. I was cordial to them, which was borderline flirtatious. I also accepted a few drink offers here and there. Davin appeared to remain calm and cool throughout the night, but that all changed once we got in the cab to get back to the hotel.

I leaned over to put my head on his shoulder and he shrugged me away. "Whoa!" I said laughing playfully as I over dramatically fell to the other side of the cab's back seat. I stopped laughing when I looked at his face and saw that he was not joining me in my amusement. "What's wrong?" I asked sincerely because I truly did not know.

He was quiet for a while before he finally answered "You've changed." I wasn't sure where he was going with this, so I waited to see if he had anything to add to that statement.

After another long pause he went on to say, "You are not the same girl that I met and fell in love with. You used to be kind, nice and innocent. Now you are self absorbed and never satisfied. You don't care about other people as much as you try to act like you do."

I was floored. I had no clue that he felt this way. I was hurt.

"Davin, where is this coming from?"

He let out a deep sigh and said. "See, that's what I mean. This is news to you, but I have been feeling this way for a while now.

The Ups and Downs of Being Round
Monica Marie Jones

You are proving my point exactly because you have been too busy exercising, working and hanging out with your new friends in Detroit to even notice. Then you come home and throw it all up in my face. You brag about how much fun you are having and how much attention you are getting. Do you think I want to hear that all of the time? No, especially when I am not having fun. I've am working my butt off trying to pay for our wedding. While you are losing all this weight and looking all great, have you noticed that I have gained quite a bit of weight? How do you think it makes me feel that now you are all fit and fabulous and I am sitting back getting fat and frustrated?"

I couldn't believe it. I was speechless. I didn't even know what say in response. I could see his point, but one thing stood out to me. I didn't want to believe it to be true, but Davin was jealous of me. He had gained weight, but like most guys, I never thought that he was self conscious about it.

My lifestyle change and weight loss were rewarding but it was a very difficult time for me emotionally. I needed the support and understanding of my friends, family and loved ones more than ever. I was angry at Davin. The one time in our relationship that I tried to do something for myself he wasn't able to be there for me. I had always been there for him - from washing his dirty drawers to helping him with papers when he was in school. I didn't do it to get anything in return, but at this time in my life, I needed him to be happy for me and he couldn't give me that.

I decided not to respond. We rode back to the hotel in silence. I'm not sure that he cared what I thought on the subject. That night a change occurred in what we had. Resentment set in our relationship. It fed off our insecurities and it grew bigger by the day.

As my resentment for Davin grew, I began plunged deeper into the downward spiral of destructive behavior.

Since Davin and I lived together, I felt smothered in my own home. That led me to find more reasons to work late or hang out with my friends in Detroit. I also found myself drinking more and finding more guys to cheat on Davin with.

After that first encounter with Tone, we kept it going for a while, but I found myself bored with him, especially when he started to talk about us getting serious. That took all of the fun out of it for me. I already had a fiancé, why would I want to get serious with someone else? He didn't get it, so it was time to move on. Besides, I had become curious about all of these other men that had been trying to pursue me. I had replaced my destructive behavior of eating to cope with drinking and sex. I started to become desensitized and detached from all of my feelings and emotions. I was still hungry, but I no longer used food to satisfy my hunger.

It began to become difficult to keep my dual existence separate. I longed for the excitement of my life in Detroit most of the time. When I was at home, I would spend countless hours on the computer chatting and emailing my friends in Detroit. I would send them detailed accounts of the daring trysts and escapades that would go on behind Davin's back. I wrote one email in particular that was so vivid that it read like a chapter from a steamy romance novel, so I saved it. Perhaps it could be of use at a later date.

More loss

The Ups and Downs of Being Round
Monica Marie Jones

A few weeks later I was on my commute to work when Davin called me on my cell phone. He didn't bother giving me the satisfaction of the greeting when I answered the phone. He cut right to the chase.

"Madison, are you cheating on me?" In an attempt to stall for time to think of a response I said "Huh?" I knew full well that I had heard him loud and clear. He caught me completely off guard and I needed time to regroup. Unable to think of what to say and not wanting to volunteer too much information, I quickly followed that "Huh?" with the most convincing "No!" that I could muster.

"Madison. I am going to give you one more chance to stop the lies. ARE YOU CHEATING ON ME?" He said more sternly this time. I refused to let my guard down. I was going to deny the truth as long as I possibly could. We had been growing apart, but I did not want to break up. As stupid as I had been acting by leading my double life in Detroit, I knew that I had a good thing. I figured that I was just going through a phase and once I got it out of my system, I would be ready to get married. In all of my extra curricular dating, I had yet to find a man that was as good as or better than Davin, so I didn't want to lose him. I was comfortable.

"Davin, What are you talking about?" I said in a calm and even tone trying my best to appear unfazed by his interrogation. "Ok. So I see you are not going to make this easy. I tried to give you one last chance to be honest with me, but you couldn't even give me that. You are more far gone than I thought."

I didn't know what to think. If he had found out something, what was it and how did he know? I had been careful to cover my

The Ups and Downs of Being Round
Monica Marie Jones

tracks. And since Davin wasn't from Detroit, I was sure that there was no way he could know someone there that I was messing around with. I continued to play dumb. If the truth was going to come out, I wasn't going to be the one to reveal it.

"Look, Davin, I don't have any idea what you are talking about." I said, adding attitude to my tone. I figured that if I was going to try to stand my ground, I might as well try to sound as convincing as possible. "Madison! Do I need to replay the vivid details for you? Will that refresh your memory?" Not knowing where he was going, I remained silent.

"Ok, fine. It was late on a hot summer night, and it was just you and him at the park...." At that moment it hit me - Davin read my email.

Instead of feeling bad or guilty, my initial reaction was anger. "Davin! You read my email? How dare you violate my privacy like that? "I yelled into the phone. I was fully prepared to continue my rant when he cut me off by responding in a quiet, monotone voice on the brink of being emotional, "How dare you violate my health, our engagement...my trust?" That question was met with complete silence, on both of our ends.

About two minutes passed. I pulled over on the shoulder of the highway because I was no longer able to concentrate on driving. My tear filled eyes made visibility impossible. The silence was broken by Davin's voice.

"Madison. Its over. I need you to move out. I can't be around you another moment. Let me know when you are coming to move your things so I can plan NOT to be there." Click.

The Ups and Downs of Being Round
Monica Marie Jones

I tried calling him back several times but each time the calls went straight to his voicemail. That was for the best because I had no idea what to say. I just sat there on the side of the road and cried until an officer pulled up to see if everything was ok.

There was no sense in fighting it. I was wrong and I didn't deserve Davin. I couldn't even face him after he had read that email. The details were so vivid that I am certain that he became physically sick after reading them. If I read an email like that about him and another woman, I probably would have vomited on the spot.

I left Davin a message letting him know the date and time that I would be coming to get my stuff. I called my uncle who had a few rental properties in the city to arrange for a place to stay temporarily until I got my own place. Out of all of the guys I was messing around with in Detroit, none of them had their own place, so staying with them wasn't an option. Jaynelle and her man had just gotten a place together and I was not about to be the third wheel, so that was out. As much as I loved my Mom, I was just too far beyond going back to live at home. If I could have seen myself living with anyone it would have been my little brother Ryan Jr, but at that point he had joined the military and moved down South.

Davin and I had purchased a lot of furniture, appliances and other luxuries together, but I left it all behind. I got all of my clothes and bare necessities and decided to start over from scratch. This would not be so easy. Many of our purchases and bills were in my name and we had a joint bank account. There were still a lot of things that tied us together. Communication was going to be inevitable at some point.

CHAPTER 13

Reflection

Living on my own in Detroit was not all it was cracked up to be. Now that I was actually living here, it wasn't the exciting escape like it used to be. Since I wasn't sneaking and living a dual life, the thrill had faded and fizzled out. Now that I had all of this extra free time, my friends in Detroit didn't seem to be as available to me as they were when I was creeping from Ypsilanti. They actually had real lives and jobs of their own. Their sole responsibility was not feeding my need for pleasure.

Reality set in and I became a single woman living on my own. I realized how much I had taken for granted having Davin around to keep me company, help me out with the bills, and give me a feeling of safety and security. I had lost touch with who I was as an individual.

What was my favorite food? What did I like to do in my spare time? What was my passion in life? I thought long and hard but I really couldn't answer those questions. I didn't know the answers because I had become so wrapped up in my relationship that I had lost all sense of myself. Who was I? It was clearly time to reacquaint myself with me.

I incorporated long walks in the park and journal writing into my fitness plan which provided time and space to think and process my thoughts. I posed and answered several questions in an attempt to get to know myself better. The harsh reality hit me that there were still a lot of things that I didn't like about myself that I really needed to change.

The Ups and Downs of Being Round
Monica Marie Jones

With my life completely turned upside down, the only thing that I had going for me was that I wasn't fat anymore. It was a nice feeling. I felt better about myself, I had more energy and I got tons of attention. But something was still missing. I did not feel happy and whole like I thought I would. I had shed 70 pounds, but it still felt like I had a ton of baggage weighing down my heart.

I have heard many people say, "if I could just lose weight, I would be happy." But I realized that there is so much more to it than that. Yes, I lost the weight, but in the process I also lost my fiancé, and my self-respect, because I engaged in behaviors that weren't good. Is that the necessary price I had to pay? Or could I have gone about it all in a better way? And what was still missing? What was I still hungry for?

I pondered these thoughts as I walked into my fitness center. I had reached my two-year anniversary mark at the center and had been an inspiration to many. My before- and-after pictures were posted on the walls to motivate other members. My friends and family had joined me in my journey to fitness and had become successful in losing weight and leading healthier lives. Even though I felt like crap, a lot of good had come out of the situation.

I changed into my workout gear and began my usual routine. Five minutes into my workout, I had the undeniable feeling that someone was watching me. I looked around in an attempt to confirm this gut feeling and I saw a young lady that looked to be a few years younger than me watching my every move. She was considerably overweight and it seemed to take a tremendous amount of effort for her to keep up with the exercises. I could tell from her lack of familiarity with the equipment that this was probably her first day there.

When our eyes met, she contemplated something then with some hesitancy approached me. When she got to me, she introduced herself and said timidly, "sorry to interrupt your workout. I hope you don't mind me asking, but you're so thin, why are you here?"

Here question brought a smile to my face and sparked the beginning of a new stage of my life as I ventured out into the world on my own on the "flip side of fat."

Afterword

    This story is truly a testimony because while it is a work of fiction, I truly experienced what was like to be overweight and successfully lose that weight by changing my lifestyle. I not only write to process my emotions and to share my experiences, but I write because I want to help people change their lives for the better and become the best they can be. For that reason I have included the non fiction account of how I really changed my lifestyle and lost the weight as well as a poem I wrote when it was all said and done to help me stay on track emotionally.

    I also came to realize what that unending hunger was that I mentioned throughout the book. There was clearly a void in my life and I tried to fill it with food first. Once I was able to break the unhealthy habit of emotional eating, I fell into other destructive behaviors.

    When I was near my whit's end, almost having destroyed myself physically, mentally and emotionally, I finally realized that the only thing that could curb that hunger, quench that thirst and fill that void, had been available to me all along. That thing being a relationship with God.

    Use this plan and make it work for you. Use the poem as motivation. I hope that you are as successful in your journey as I was and continue to be. Enjoy!

Lifestyle Change

By Monica Marie Jones, M.S.W.

Introduction

Three years ago I decided to change my life. I did a lot of thinking, researching and soul searching. Once my mind was made up, I took all of the necessary steps to accomplish my goals. I joined Curves for women, changed my eating habits and lifestyle and stuck with it. The journey has been hard and challenging and it is not over yet, but I have been extremely blessed and successful. To date I have lost 65lbs and 56.75 inches and nine dress sizes. What is most rewarding about the whole process is that I did it the right way. No gimmicks, no pills, no drinks, no fad diets, and no surgery. This is not a diet. This is a life style change. I may not be an expert in the fields of fitness and nutrition, but this is what I did, and what I did has worked for me.

Monica's Daily Meal Plan

Breakfast

This meal should be eaten as soon as you wake up, ideally between the hours of 7:00am and 10:00am. A whole grain, high fiber cereal with fat free skim milk (Wheaties, Bran flakes, Cheerios, oatmeal, mini wheats, Kashi…basically anything that says wheat or bran). This should be enough if you are on the go, but if you have the time and you are still hungry, you can add fruit or low fat yogurt to your breakfast menu. If you feel the need for meat or protein try boiled eggs or an egg white omelet, turkey bacon, or turkey sausage. Make sure you drink at least two 8 oz servings of water.

Tips:

If you are going to do it big at any meal, this is the best because you have all day to burn it off.

There are two 8 oz servings of water in the standard 16 oz bottle of water.

Morning Snack

The morning snack should be consumed two to three hours after breakfast. All of your daily snacks should be something that can fit in the palm of your hand. Carbohydrate snacks should be consumed earlier in the day and before and after workouts. Some options for your morning snack include: *Fruits* (grapes, *strawberries, *blueberries, *raspberries, *cantaloupe, raisins, small apples, oranges, bananas, grapefruit, honey dew melon, pineapple, peaches, watermelon, dried fruit, etc.)

*Indicates fruits that are lower in sugar and carbohydrates.

Vegetables (celery, cucumber, broccoli, cauliflower, baby carrots, peppers, grape tomatoes, V8, etc), *yogurt* (Dannon makes a great low carb yogurt), *nuts* (pistachios, sun flower seeds, cashews, almonds, trail mix, peanuts) try to go for unsalted when it comes to the nuts. Beware of trail mixes that have candy in them and pay attention to the serving sizes because nuts are very high in calories. *Granola or Breakfast Bars (*Nature Valley and Quaker are good brands) be sure that the bars are more on the natural side (whole grains, low fat, etc). Some bars trick you because they are packed with calories, sugar and carbs. Read the labels. If they have chocolate in them they are probably not your best choice. Make sure you drink at least two 8 oz servings of water.

Tips:

If you are a busy person, pack a goodie bag the night before that contains all of the snacks and meals that you will need for the day. Pre-package everything in small serving sizes by using snack sized zip lock baggies.

The Ups and Downs of Being Round
Monica Marie Jones

To make sure that you are getting your 8 to 10 glasses of water each day, keep a case of bottled water in your trunk and or at your job.

Lots of foods that claim to be healthy are really tricky. Be sure to read the labels carefully. Look for the calories, the carbohydrates, the sugars, the fat, and the sodium. Also pay close attention to what they consider to be one serving. We may eat an entire bag of chips thinking that since it said 200 calories then that is all that we consumed. If you read the labels closely, you may find that in some bags and containers of food as many as 10 servings - 10 x 200=2000. You just consumed more than enough calories for an entire day in one sitting.

Lunch

Lunch should be consumed two to three hours after your morning snack. Lunch options include: A chicken, turkey or tuna salad, or sandwich. On the salad, omit the croutons, cheese, bacon and creamy dressings if possible. Try using vinaigrette dressing instead. (Raspberry, olive oil, balsamic, Italian etc.) Sandwiches should be on 100% whole wheat or whole grain bread that has 3 grams of fiber or more per serving. Fruit, vegetables, and or yogurt can be used as sides for your lunch. Make sure you drink at least two 8 oz servings of water.

Tips:

Take a multi vitamin at some point throughout the day, preferably with a meal, after exercising.

You always want to eat within an hour after exercising. Your body needs fuel that has sugar, carbs and fat. After strength training, you want to make sure to eat something that has protein. Many of the snack options above and below are good for post work-out snacks.

Get your salad dressing on the side, dip your fork in the dressing, then spear your salad to avoid using too much salad dressing

Afternoon Snack

The afternoon snack should be consumed two to three hours after lunch. This snack is pretty much the same as the morning snack (see above). The only difference is that you want to go a little lighter on the carbs if possible because now you are more than halfway through your day, which gives you less time to burn it off. The only exception is if you exercise at night. In that case carbs are fine because you need that energy to use during your work out. Make sure you drink at least two 8 oz servings of water.

Tips:

I take herbal laxative pills or laxative tea once a month to rid my body of excess waste and to promote regularity.

Healthy snacks that satisfy your sweet tooth include: peanut butter and jelly sandwich on whole wheat bread, toast with sugar free jelly on whole wheat bread, a spoon full of peanut butter, sugar free hot chocolate, herbal tea with honey, fat free pudding, sugar free Jell-O with fat free Cool Whip, fruit cocktail, Peaches / pineapple /

cantaloupe with cottage cheese, apple slices with fat free caramel dip, fat free frozen yogurt, sugar free ice cream, apple slices with fat free cream cheese mixed with brown sugar and chopped walnuts as a dip, raisins, Craisins (dried cranberries), trail mix, low fat yogurt, granola bars, and cereal bars.

Dinner

Dinner should be consumed two to three hours after your afternoon snack. Dinner should be light. Options include: Lean meat (turkey, chicken, or fish) that is grilled, steamed, or baked and steamed or raw vegetables (salad, mixed vegetables, broccoli, spinach, greens, etc.) Carbohydrates should be kept to a minimum, but if they are used, they should be good carbs in small portion sizes such as brown rice, whole-wheat pasta, or beans. Make sure you drink at least two 8 oz servings of water.

Tips:

Dinner should be consumed 3 hours before bedtime. I prefer to have my last meal before 7 p.m. each day.

Drink water, herbal tea, or sugar free hot chocolate to curb late night cravings.

Brush your teeth immediately following dinner to curb your appetite.

What are good carbs?

The carbs that you want to stay away from are sweets like candy, cakes, and cookies as well as processed and refined carbs such as products made with white flour. These bad carbs include white table sugar, white pasta, white bread, white rice, and crackers. Good carbs include those found in many fruits and vegetables as well as those found in whole wheat and whole grain bread, whole grain and bran cereals, brown rice, beans, and nuts.

Small changes for success

A lot of my success was due to the fact that I made a lot of small changes. These changes included smaller portion sizes, eating when I am hungry, educating myself and slowly weaning myself off of certain foods and eventually eliminating them from my diet all together. Below you will find a list of things that you can try to wean yourself off of or eliminate.

Things to eliminate	Alternative options
White table sugar	Brown sugar, honey, splenda
White rice	Brown rice, wild rice
Candy	Dried fruit, trail mix
Cake	Peanut butter and jelly sandwich
Cookies	Granola bars
Crackers	Whole wheat crackers
White Pasta	Whole wheat pasta
White bread	100% whole wheat or multi grain bread
Sugary Cereal	Wheaties, bran flakes, oatmeal, Cheerios

The Ups and Downs of Being Round
Monica Marie Jones

Hot chocolate	Sugar free hot chocolate
Salt	Mrs. Dash, Accent
Fried Chicken (and other fried foods)	Crispy baked chicken (and other foods)
Vegetable oil and butter	Olive oil
Buttery popcorn	Air popped pop corn, rice cakes
Chips	Rice cakes, wheat crackers, baked chips
Red meat and pork	Chicken, fish, turkey, sea food and tofu
Pop and juice	Water (with lemon)

Monica's daily exercise plan

A good exercise plan consists of three important components. The components are strength training, cardio, and rest. Cardio includes running, walking, elliptical machine, stair stepper, rowing, aerobic dance, spinning and any other activity that takes oxygen and keeps your heart rate up. Strength training includes resistance training, weight lifting, and toning exercises where you use your own body weight (sit ups, crunches, and push ups.) You also want to make sure to warm up then stretch before each work out and cool down then stretch after each workout. Doing these things will help to give you a more complete and effective workout as well as helping you to avoid soreness and injury.

The Ups and Downs of Being Round
Monica Marie Jones

You want to be sure to vary your work out so that you won't get bored and so that your body will not get used to what you are doing. If you keep doing the same exercise with out switching them up or increasing the intensity you will hit a plateau. When you hit a plateau you need to increase the intensity of your work out or try something different that will cause a shock to your body. If this does not work, you may need to re evaluate you eating habits. (See above list of things to reduce or give up gradually)

If your goal is to lose weight, you want to work out 5 to 6 days a week. If your goal is to maintain the weight you are at you want to work out 3 to 4 days a week. You should strength train 3 to 4 days a week with days off in between to give your muscles time to recover. You can do cardio everyday if you would like but I recommend taking it easy on your strength training days so you won't over do it. Below, you will find a sample work out plan that I do during the week.

Monday

Morning: Strength training (30 min) Curves

Evening: (optional) Calisthenics at home (Crunches and push ups)

If time permits, I will sneak in 30-45 minute on the elliptical machine at Bally's after work

Tuesday

The Ups and Downs of Being Round
Monica Marie Jones

Morning: rest

Evening: Advanced gymnastics lesson (2 hours)

Wednesday

Morning: Strength training (30 min) Curves

Evening: Hustle lessons after work

Thursday

Morning:
Run/jog two miles at the park or on the treadmill (30 minutes)
Ab/oblique/lower back work out:
- Oblique side beds with 15 lb. dumb bells

- Nautilus oblique twist machine two sets of 25 at 45lbs

- Nautilus lower back machine 2 sets of 25 at 108-120lbs

Nautilus abdominal crunch machine 2 sets of 25 at 50lbs

(Make sure to use the weight that's right for you.)

I like to work my abs, obliques and lower back areas extra for several reasons. First I have had a history of severe back problems, second I want to strengthen my core, and third that is a major problem area for me, even though I have lost a lot of weight, that area has proven to be the last to go.

Friday:

Morning: Strength training (30 min) Curves

30-45 minute on the elliptical machine, Abs/oblique/lower back work out (see Thursday)

Jump rope work out (jump 1 minute, rest one minute-3 sets of this)

Saturday

Morning: Strength training (30 min) Curves and or walk 2 to 3 miles at the park

Sunday:
REST

As you can see, some days I hit it hard, some days I take it easy. I make it a point to work out at lease 5 days at minimum and 6 days at the maximum. I always make sure to take at least one day off for rest. My daily work out may seem extreme, but it is a little more advanced because I have been doing this for three years now and I always have to kick it up a notch if I want to continue to lose weight.

The Ups and Downs of Being Round
Monica Marie Jones

Below you will find some beginner and intermediate exercises that are alternatives to the workouts that I do.

Beginner and Intermediate Exercise

Walking (on the treadmill or at the park)

Work out tapes (yoga, pilates, tae bo, aerobic dance) such as the Crunch Series is really great!

Aerobic classes at your local gym

Stationary bike

Jogging

If you feel that your schedule is too busy to squeeze in exercise, try the following tips:

Do small spurts of exercise for 10 to 15 minutes, three times a day

Go for a brisk power walk on your lunch hour

Get up an hour earlier and work out in the morning

Do an exercise tape before bed at night

Clean the house with the music on and dance while you clean

Turn on the radio or the music video channel and dance until you sweat

Do crunches, jumping jacks or push ups while you watch your favorite TV program or during the commercial

Wear a pedometer to work and try to increase the steps you take each day

Take the stairs instead of the elevator

Park father away from the entrance when you are shopping to increase walking distance

Shopping list of items that every fit person should begin to collect:

Jump rope

Dumb bells (1, 3, 5, 8, or 10lbs)

Work out videos/DVDs (Cardio, strength training, abs, Tae Bo, yoga, Pilates, dance)

Portable radio or CD player with headphones (along with some up beat/motivational music)

Yoga ball

Yoga mat

Resistance bands

Weight lifting gloves (These prevent the ugly calluses that strength training may cause)

Lots of work out gear (t-shirts, jogging pants, stretch pants, shorts, sports bras etc)

Bicycle

Roller Blades

A few good pairs of gym shoes (keep one in your car so you are always prepared)

Hula hoop

I hope that you found this information useful. It is a work in progress because like I said earlier, I am still on the journey. It will

The Ups and Downs of Being Round
Monica Marie Jones

not be easy and it will take time, but if you are serious and you stick with it, you will reach your goals.

During the last year, I found myself struggling with maintaining the weight loss, feeling discouraged and in jeopardy of gaining the weight back. Adding spiritual enrichment and a strong relationship with God to my lifestyle change plan helped everything to fall right into place and gave me the strength to continue on successfully.

If you have any questions or need any additional tips, help or support, please contact me. (monicamjones@hotmail.com). We can do this together! May you be blessed as you begin your journey!

The Ups and Downs of Being Round
Monica Marie Jones

Fat Girl

A Poem by Monica Marie Jones

A fat girl lives on the inside of me
Although I've shed the pounds
I'm still weighed down by insecurity

Mannerisms are meek and mild
Characteristics of my inner fat child

The scale and the mirror are my two biggest enemies
The scale measures failure and the mirror deceives

I don't see what others see 'cause
99% of losing weight is psychology

It has been a challenge physically
But is has been more taxing emotionally
Confusion, stress and strain afflict my psyche constantly

Put the pounds on now the weights gone
My life has become an oxymoron

When I was large I was invisible
Now that I'm small I cannot hide

The Ups and Downs of Being Round
Monica Marie Jones

At size 16 when it came to men, I was virtually unknown
At size 6 when it comes to men, they won't leave me alone

I can't help but wonder, would they acknowledge me the way I used to be?
For the majority the attraction is based solely on what they see.

Fat jokes told in my presence offend me and confuse me even more
Then I realize they're not meant for me, but for those who look how I looked before

Why is it then that they cut deep and still affect me so?
Because the fat child housed within refuses to let it go

When I shop through the aisles and look at small clothes
My inner fat child screams, "Leave those alone!"

When I try on those clothes I cannot believe
How they all fit me with elegance and ease

When I meet a new man that I catch feelings for
My inner fat child says, "When he finds out that you were fat he'll head straight for the door."

With reluctance, I reveal my past to that man
Using pictures as my evidence of my wide waist and hip span

The Ups and Downs of Being Round
Monica Marie Jones

I prepare for him to leave as she said that he would
When he surprises me by saying "girl, you still used to look good!"

"Don't believe him, he's just saying that now,
if he saw you back then he would call you a cow!"
My inner fat child says with fury and spite
putting an immediate damper on my feelings that night.

My past and my present in a constant tug-of-war
Making it hard to appreciate all I've worked so hard for

My will was strong but I could never win
Unless I confronted my demon within

I said "Fat girl, would you please just let me be?
Just let me enjoy my new healthy body."

She said "Girl don't forget that you used to be fat. You drop a few pounds now you think you all that? Just as you lost it you can gain it all back!"

I said "I'll never forget what I used to be.
I've only changed externally.
Who I am inside is the same and will always be.
Now one thing's a fact, I won't gain it all back,
I'm committed to keeping my lifestyle on track."

The Ups and Downs of Being Round
Monica Marie Jones

She said "You say that now, you gluttonous sow,

but I'll be here laughing when you finally back down."

I said, "I know that you thrive on my fear and self doubt,

I've conquered those things so now you get out.

Your nourishment comes from my insecurity,

now I am secure, so you can just leave.

You used to control everything that I'd do;

now I'm in control so I rebuke you!"

I was prepared for her response filled with vengeance and rage

After listening closely silent was all that I could gauge

Suddenly I heard a surrendering sigh

That escalated into a defeated child's cry

Those cries and small footsteps began to slowly fade away

I never heard from my inner fat child again after that day.

The Ups and Downs of Being Round
Monica Marie Jones

The Ups and Downs of Being Round

Monica Marie Jones

Made in the USA
Charleston, SC
30 March 2010